DESIGNER'S NOTEBOOK

17

BELVEDERE

LACE - VIENNA

Lace & Embroidery Patterns - Liberty Style of Vienna

ARRANGED AND EDITED BY WOLFGANG H. HAGENEY

BELVEDERE

PUBLICATIONS INTERNATIONAL, ROME/ITALY

Beauty, creativity and decoration in the lacework of Vienna's fin-de-siecle Art Nouveau

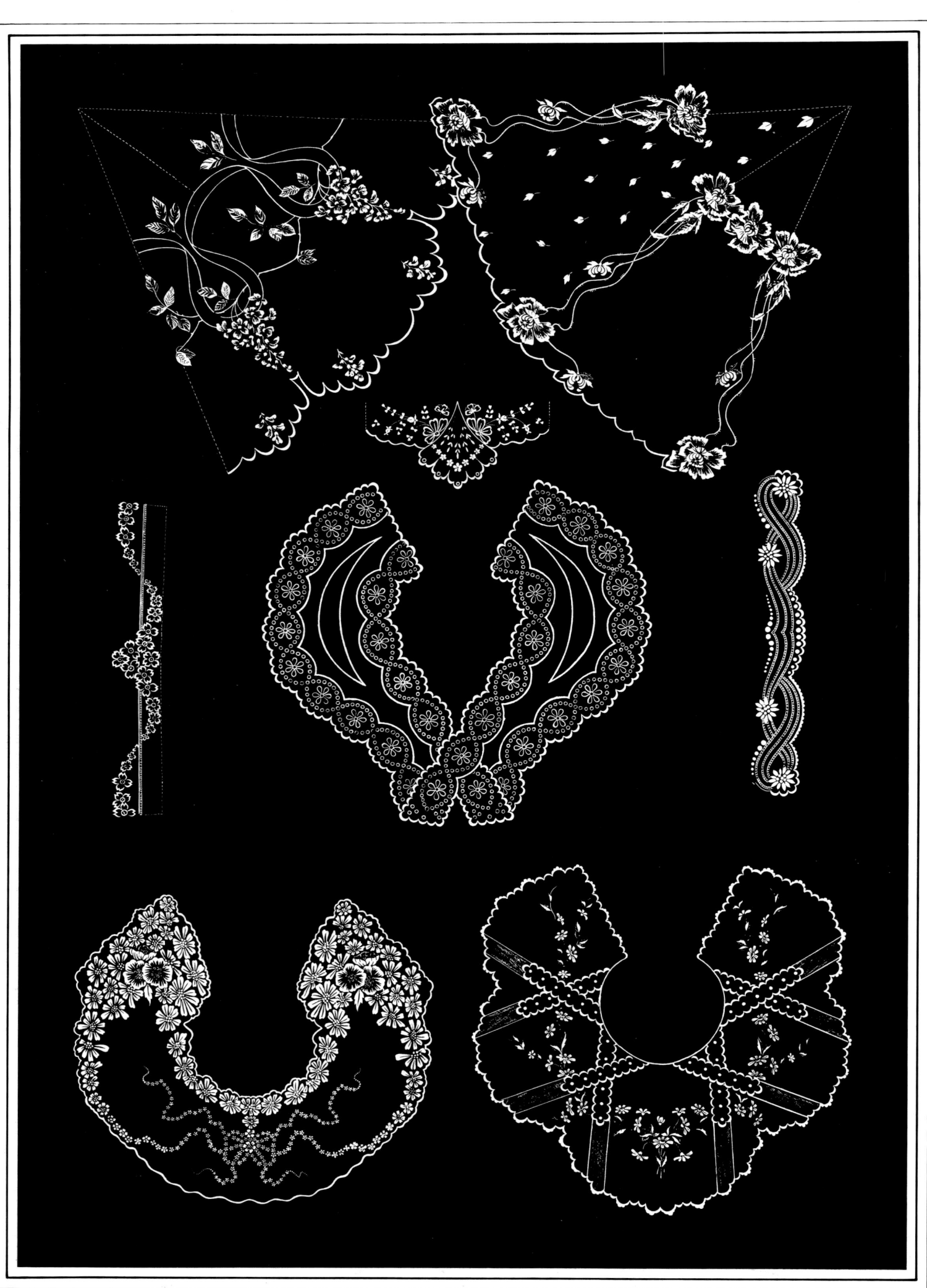

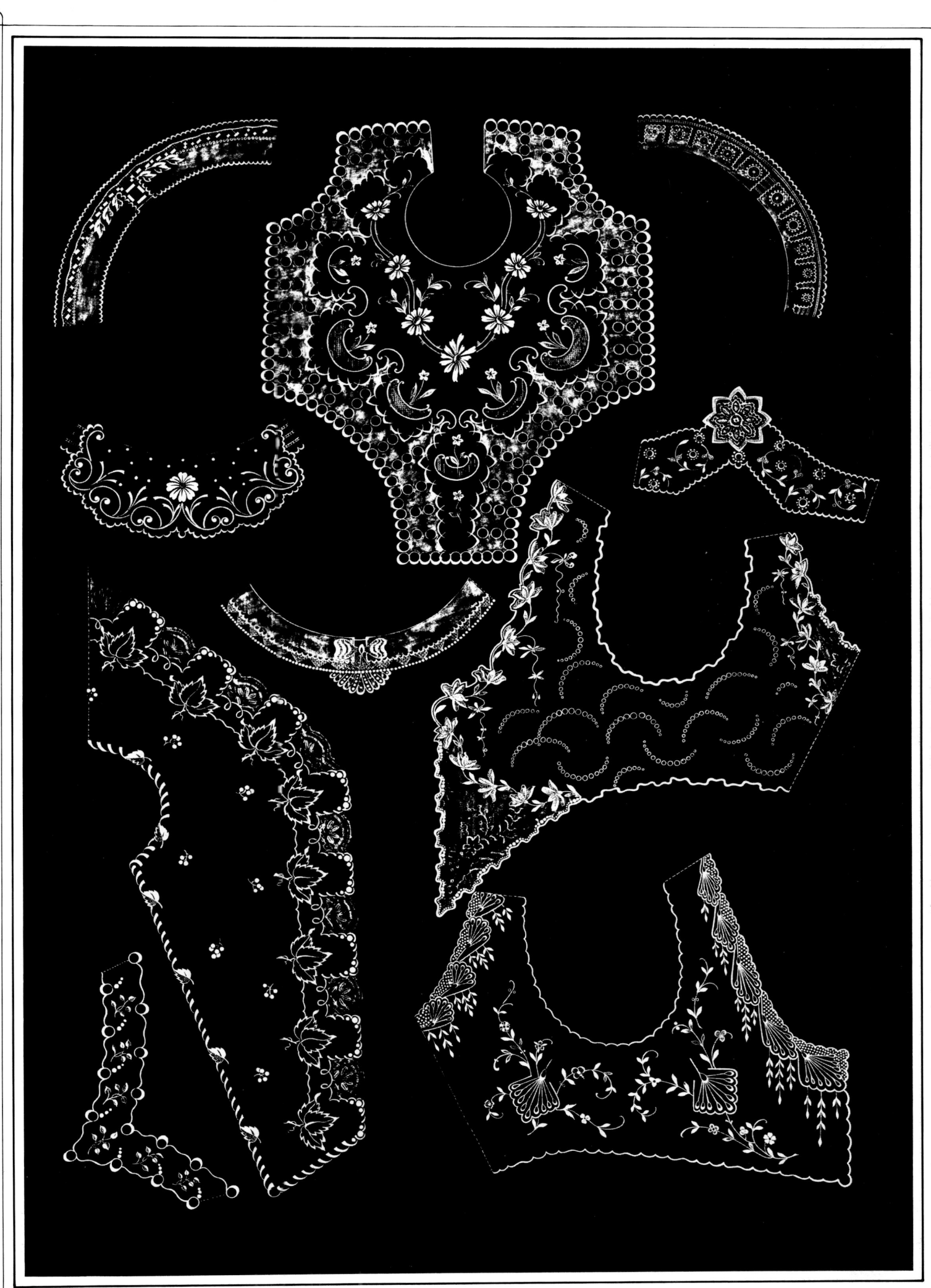

13

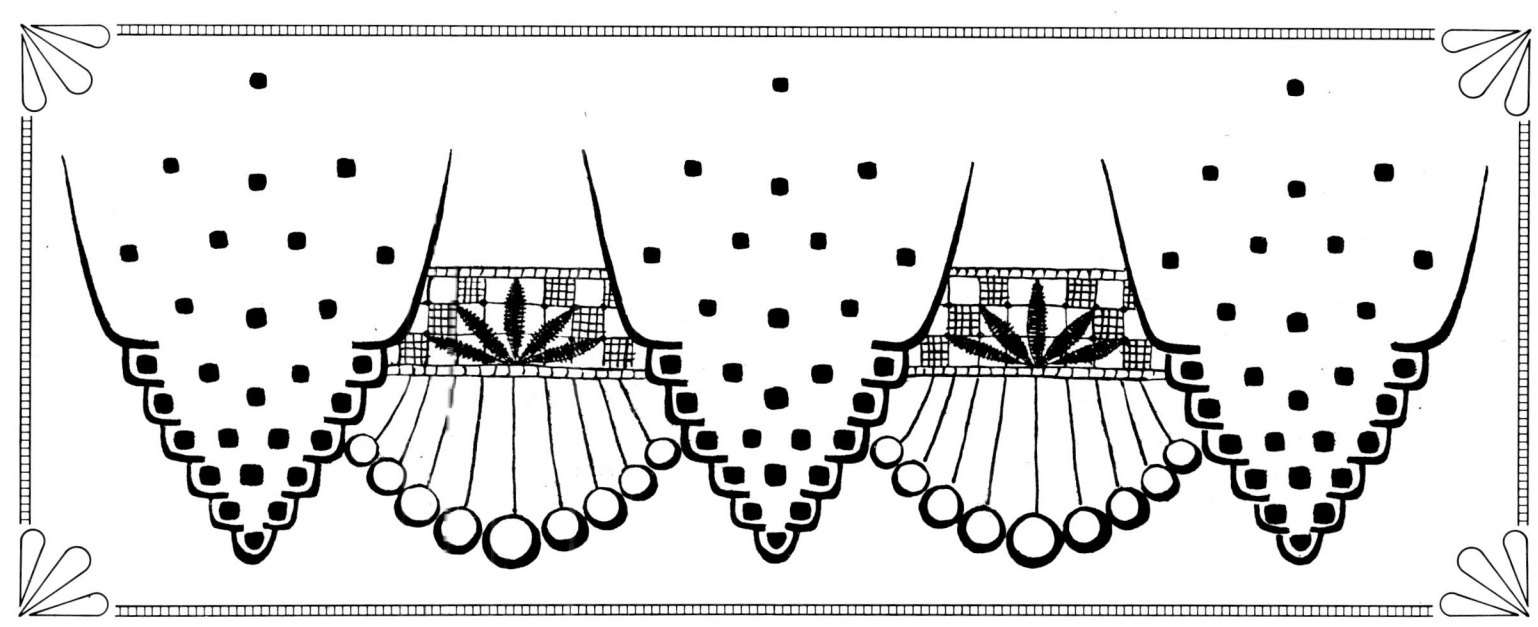

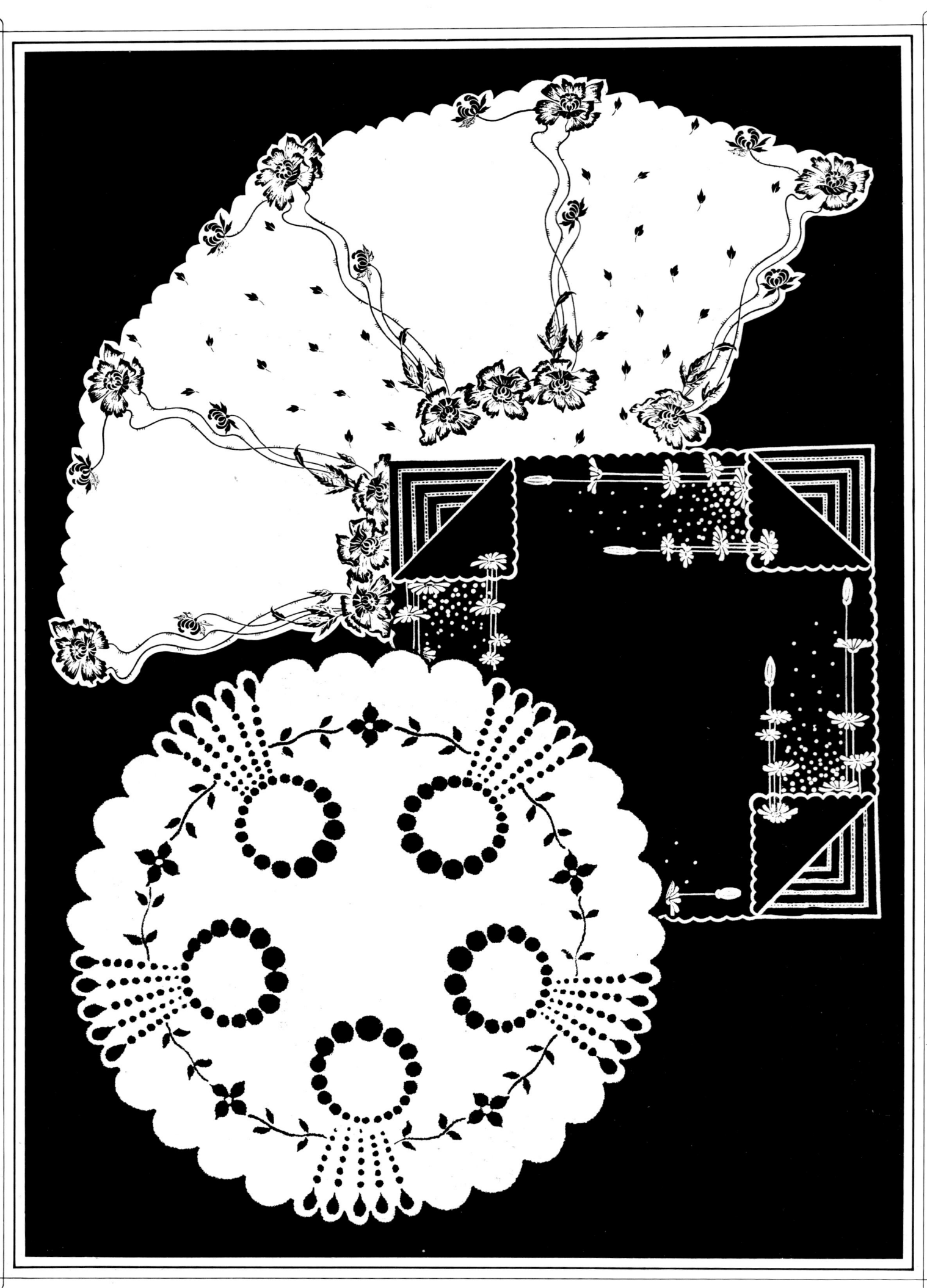

18

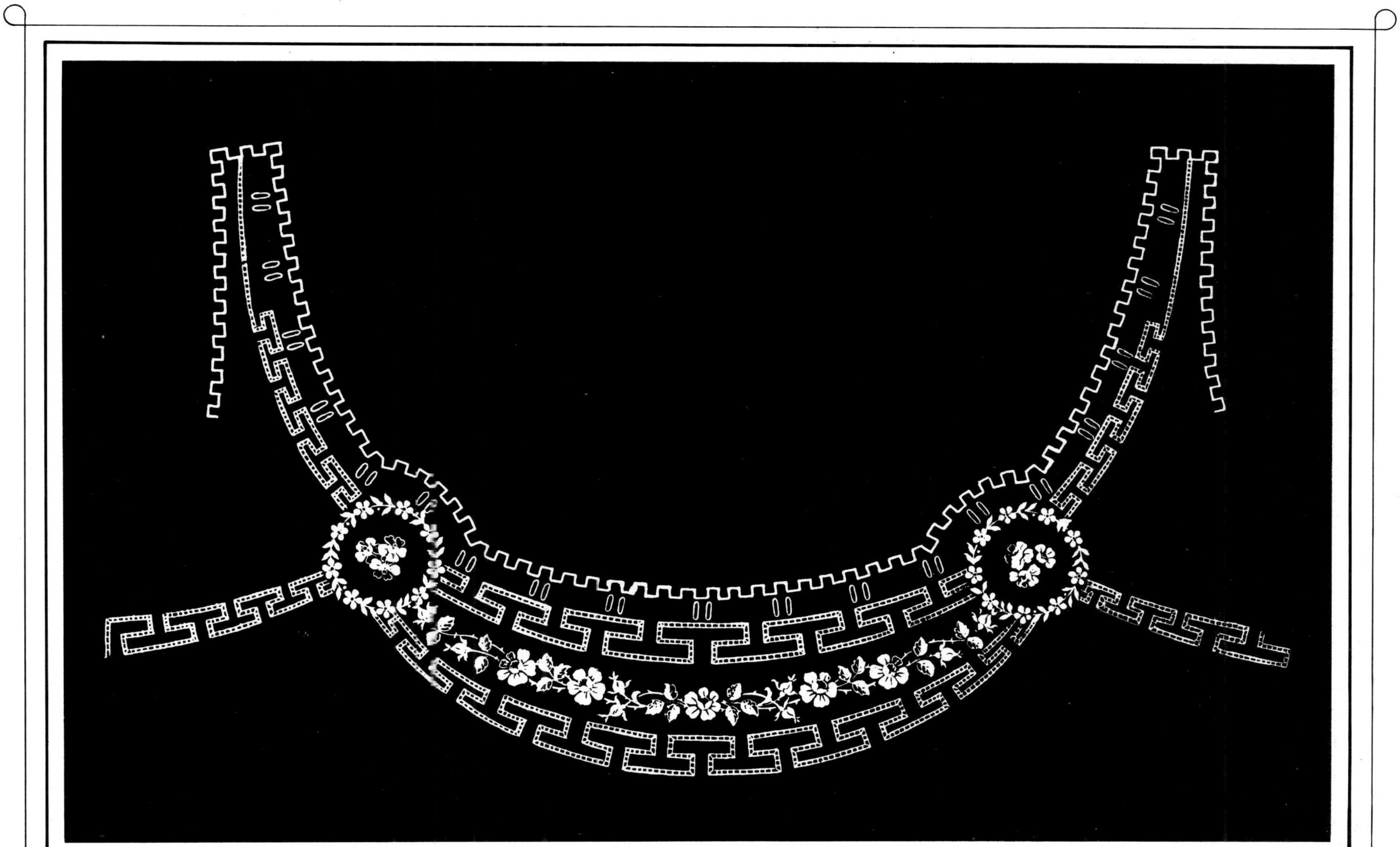

19

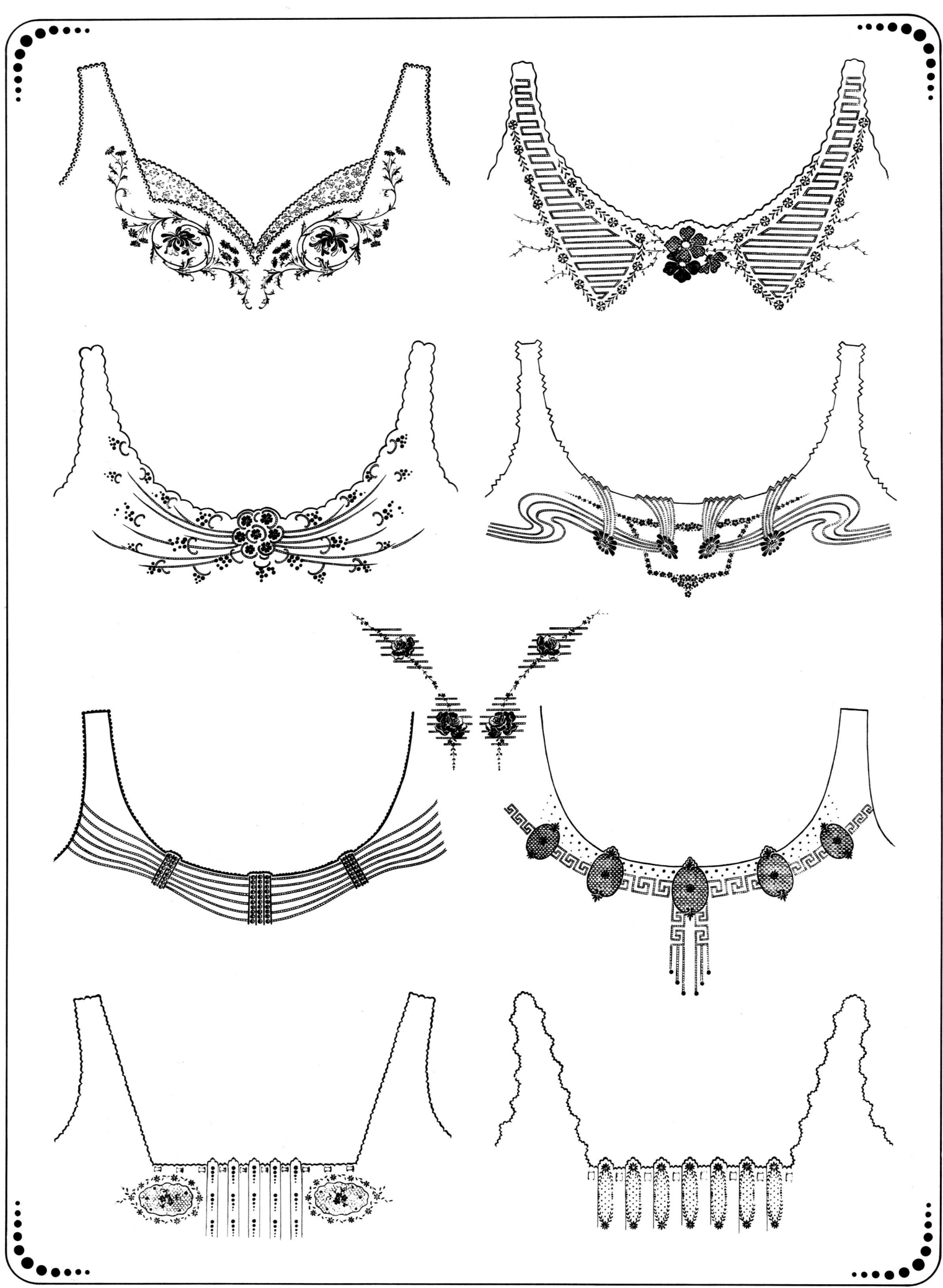

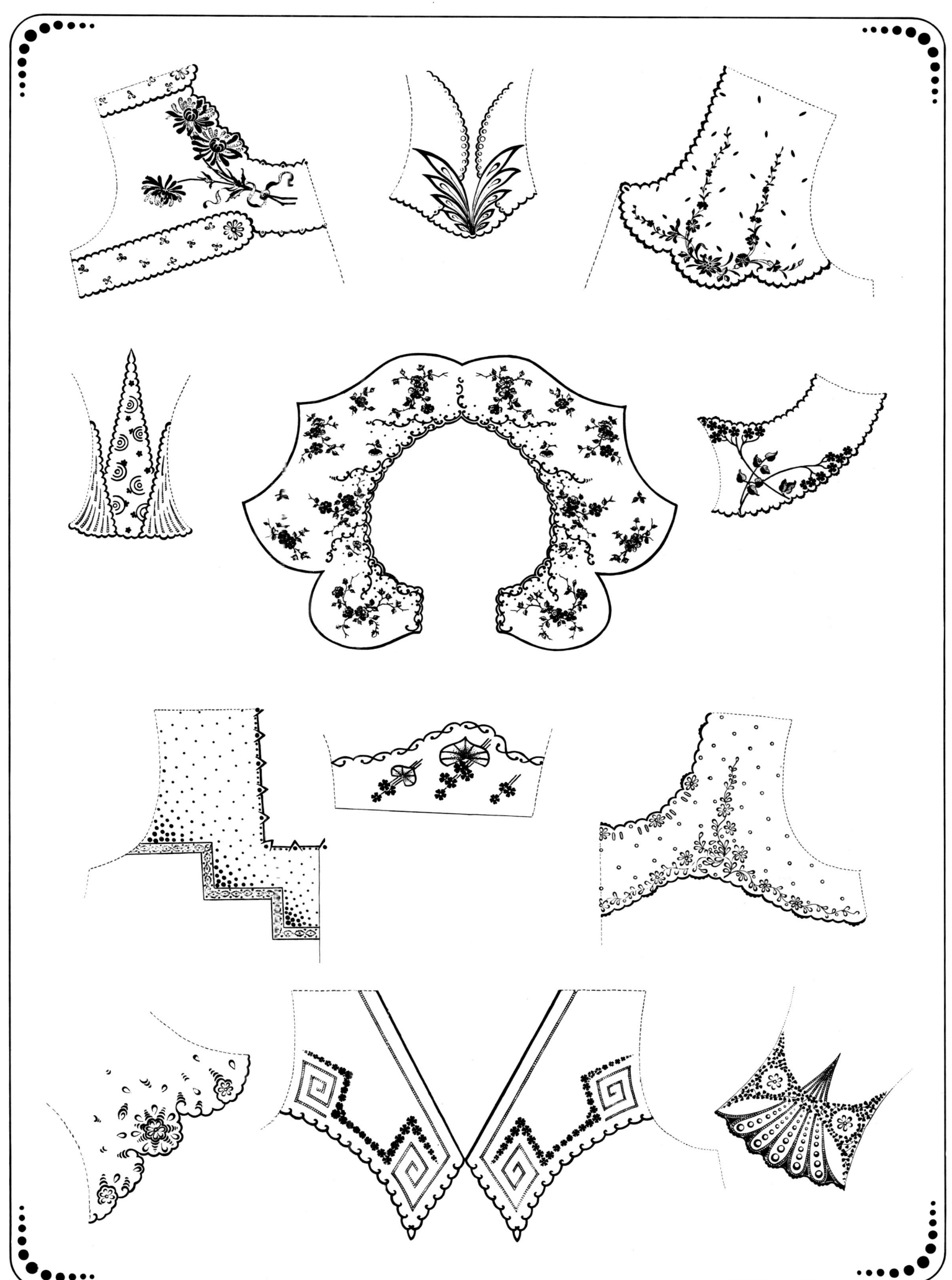

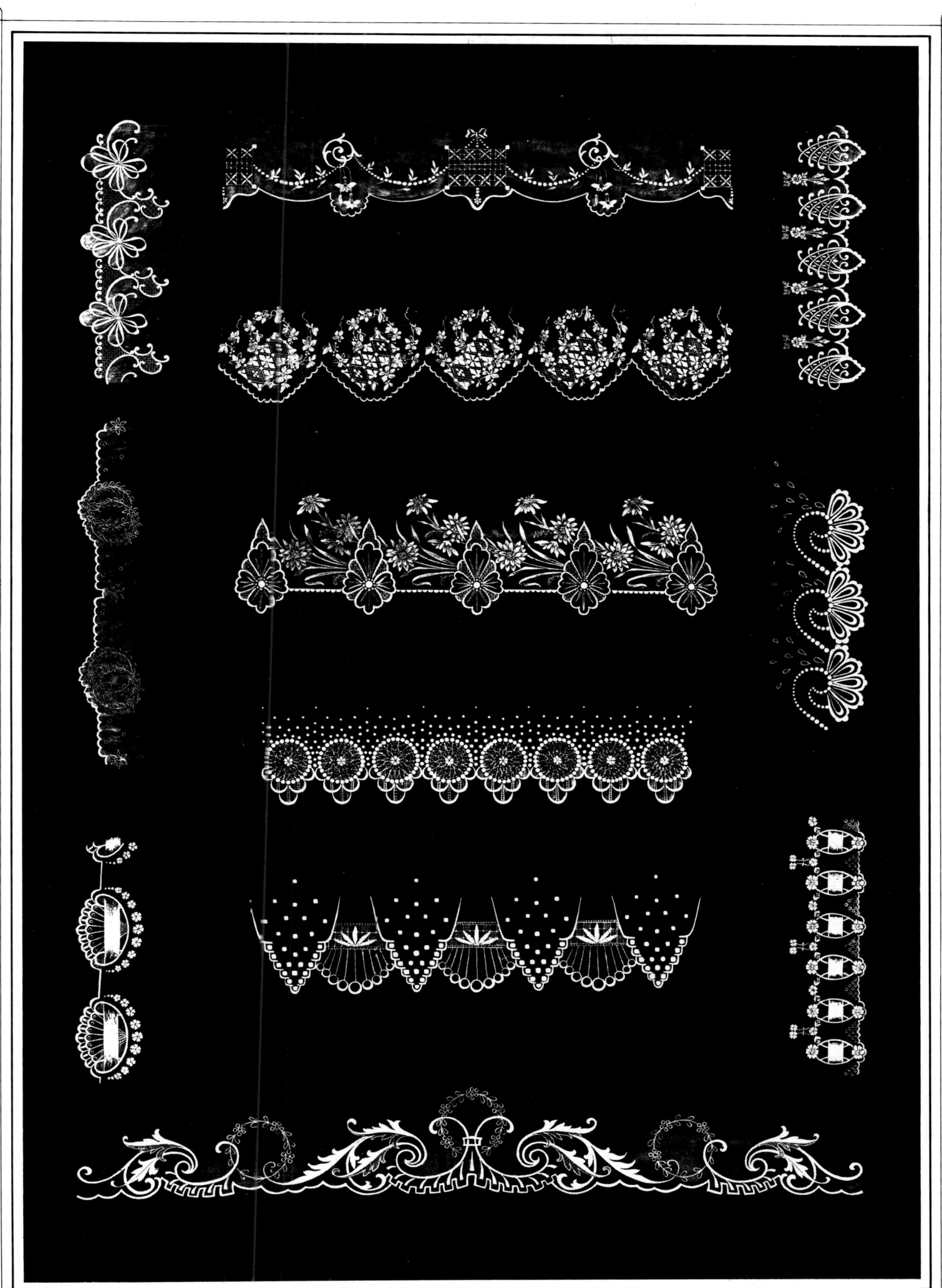

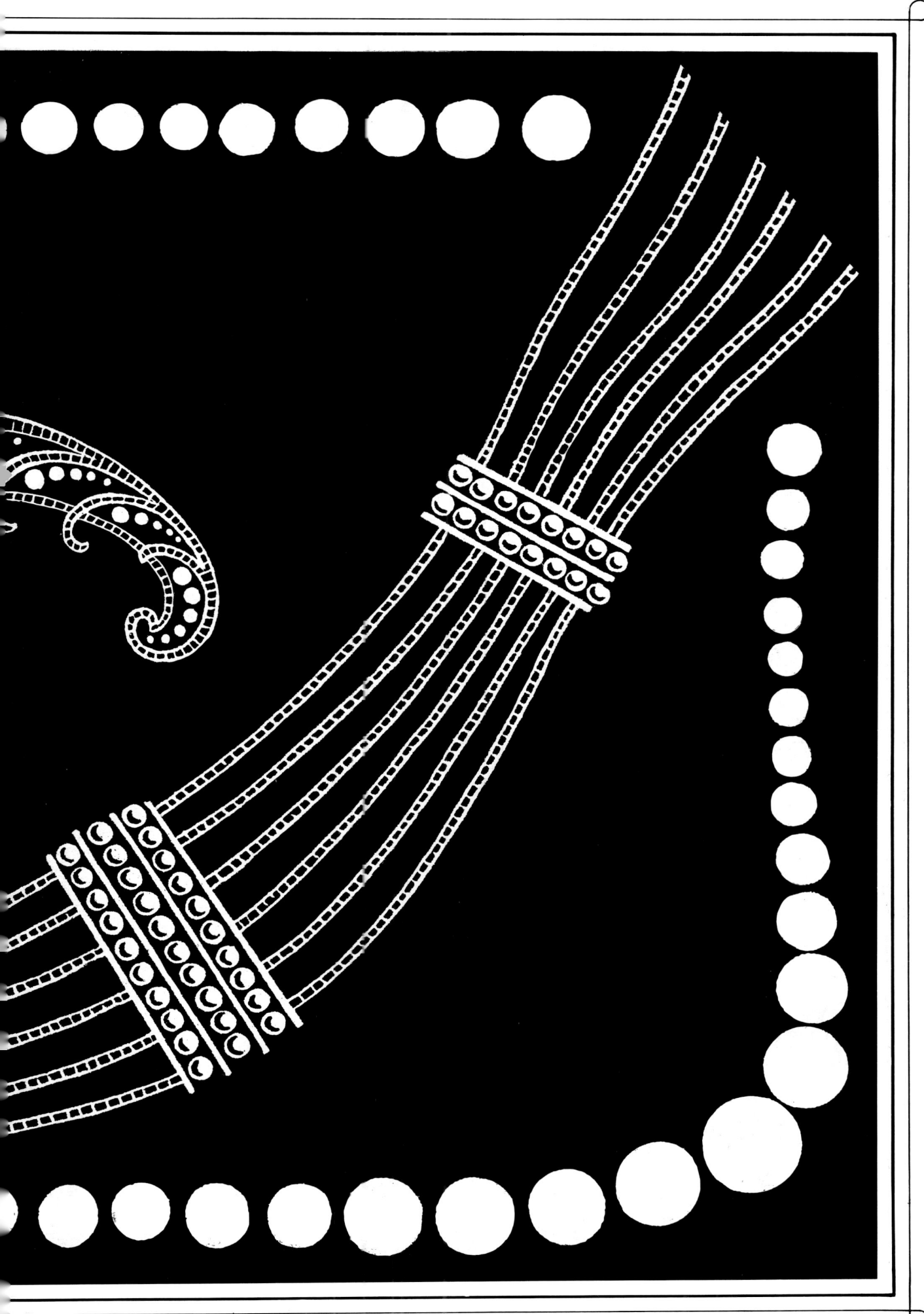

34

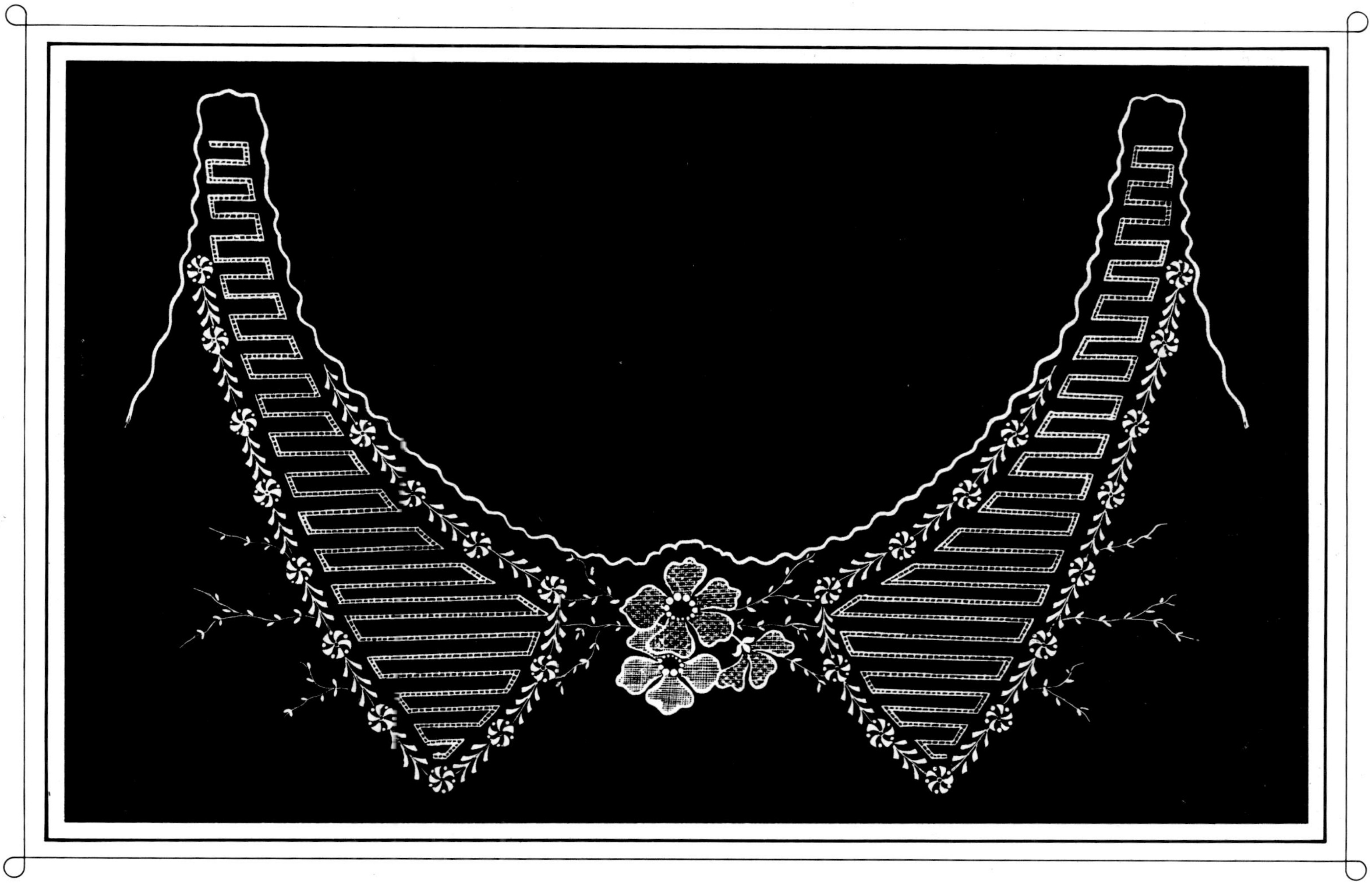

39

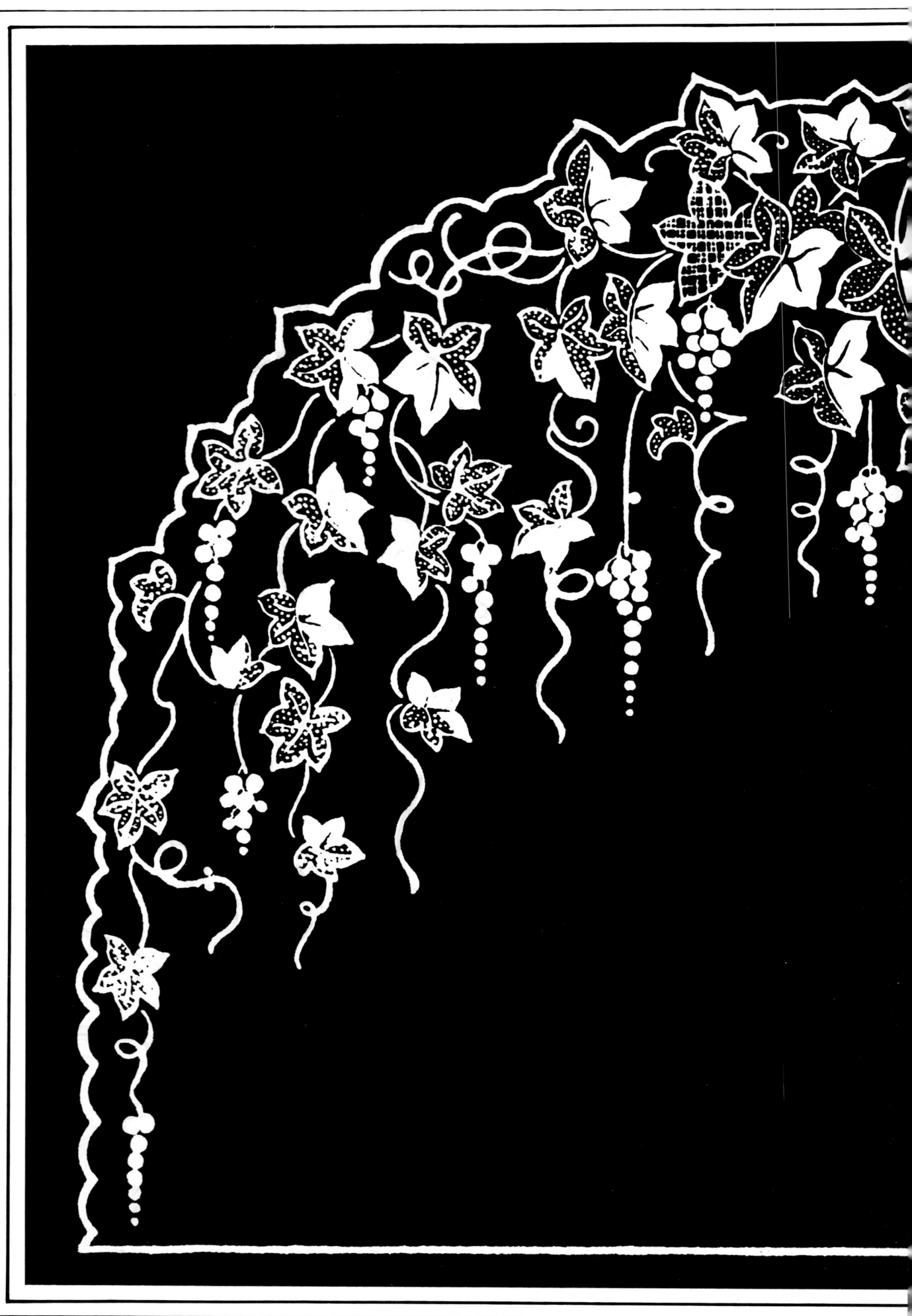

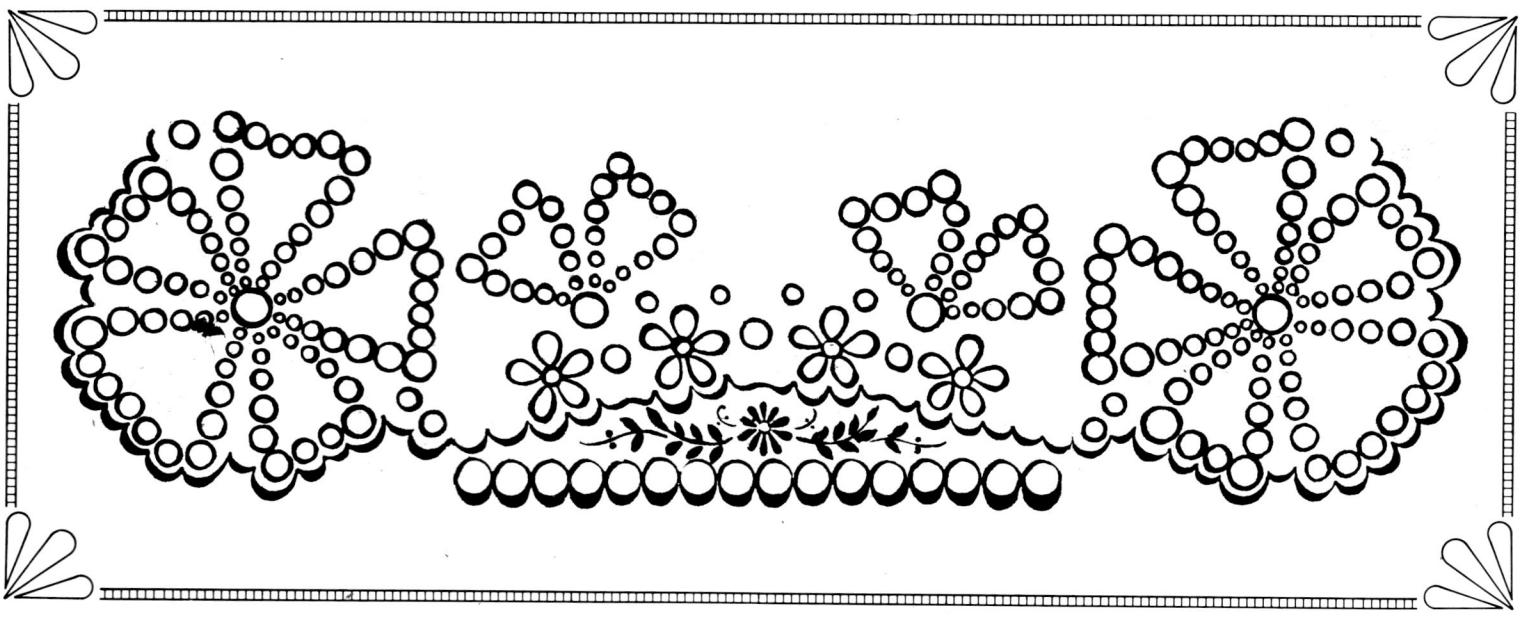

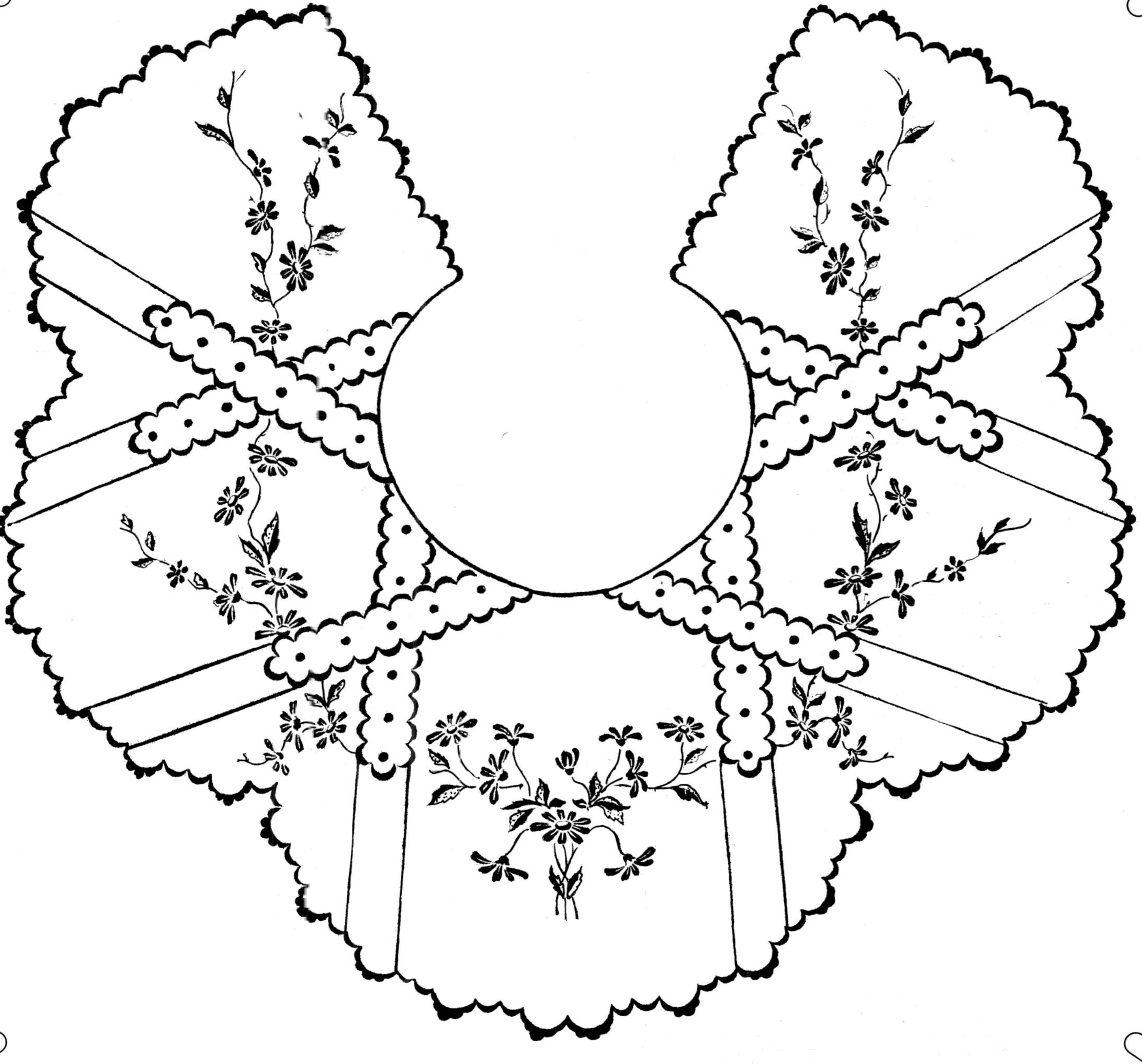

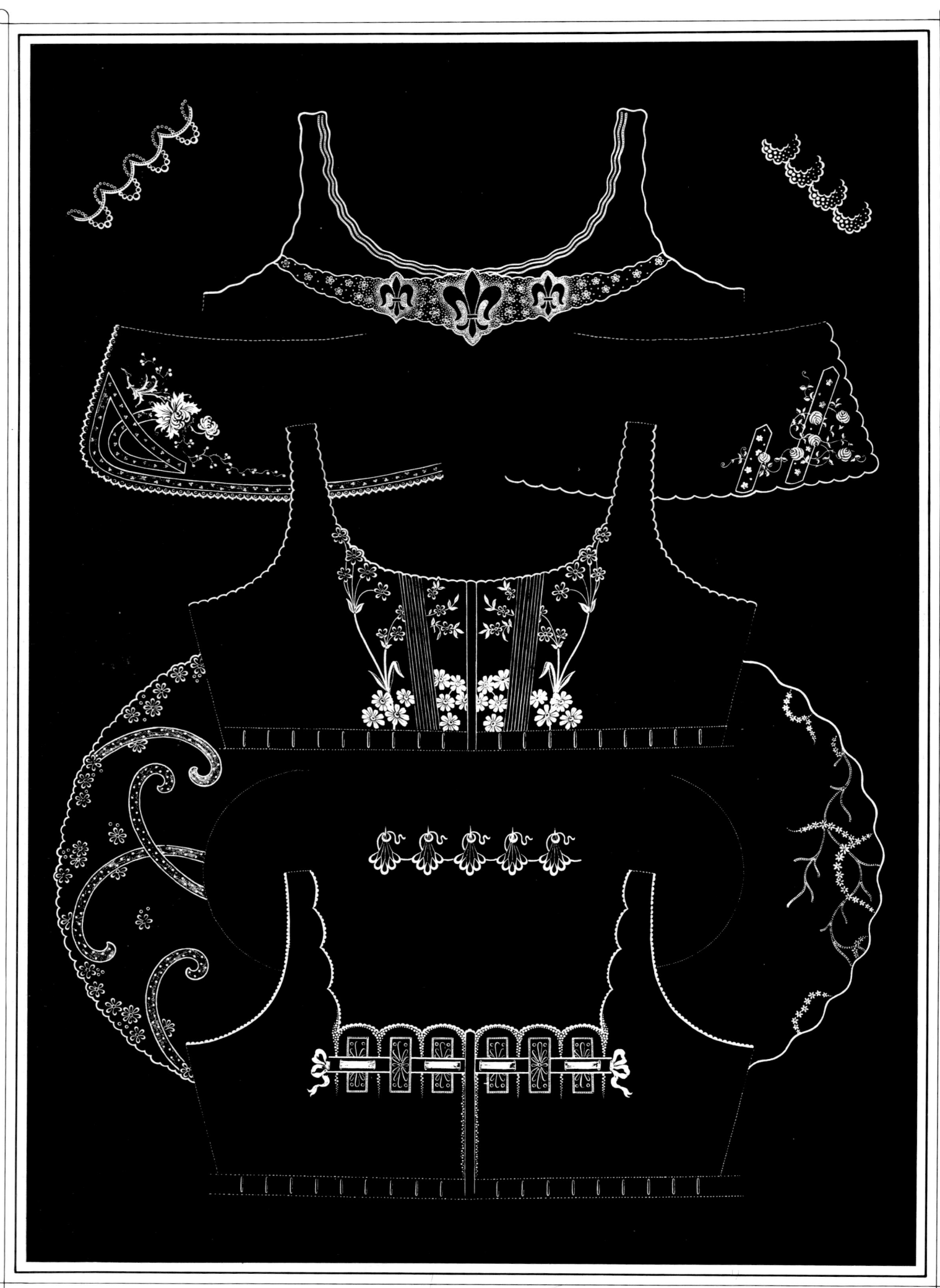

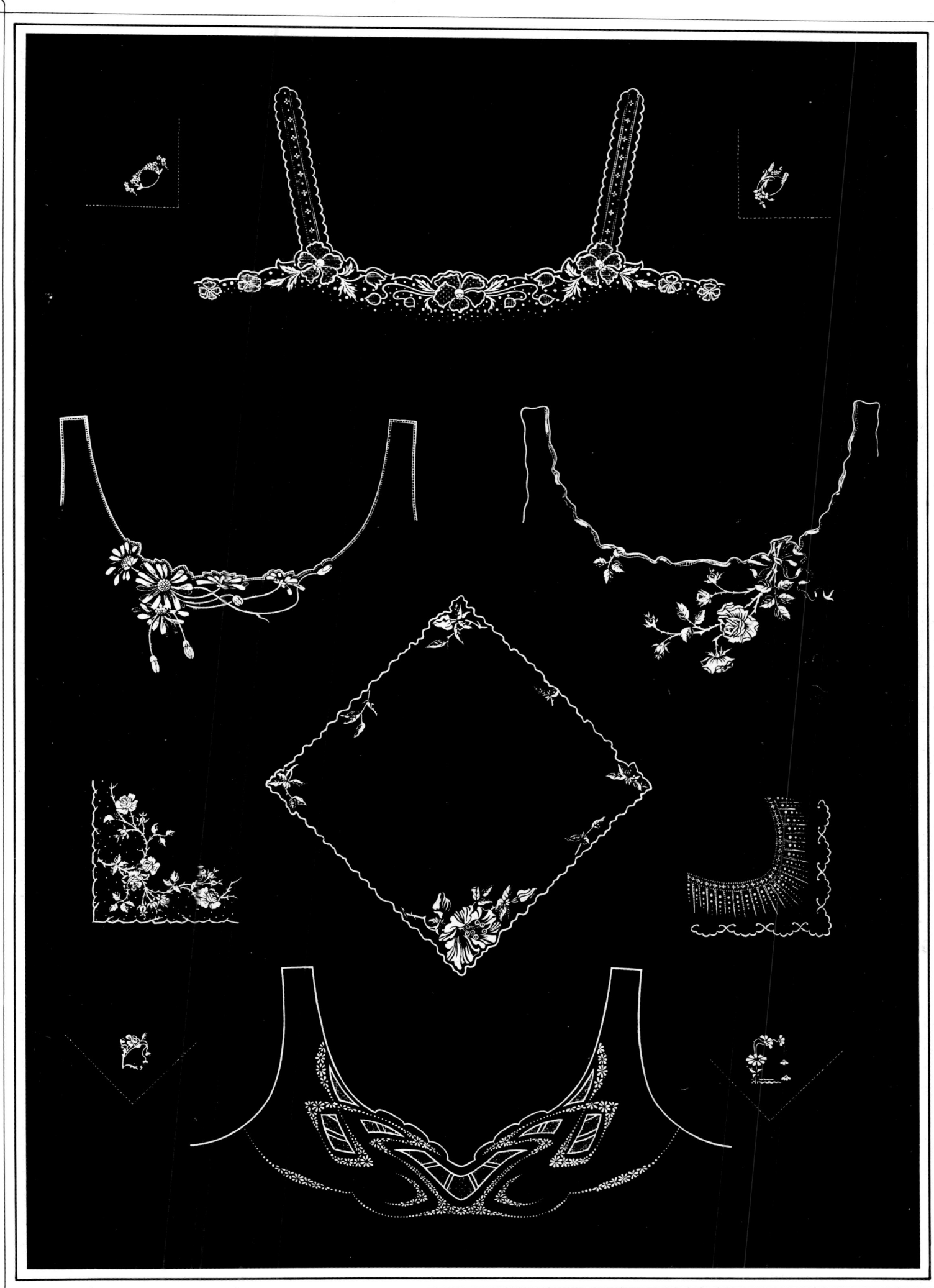

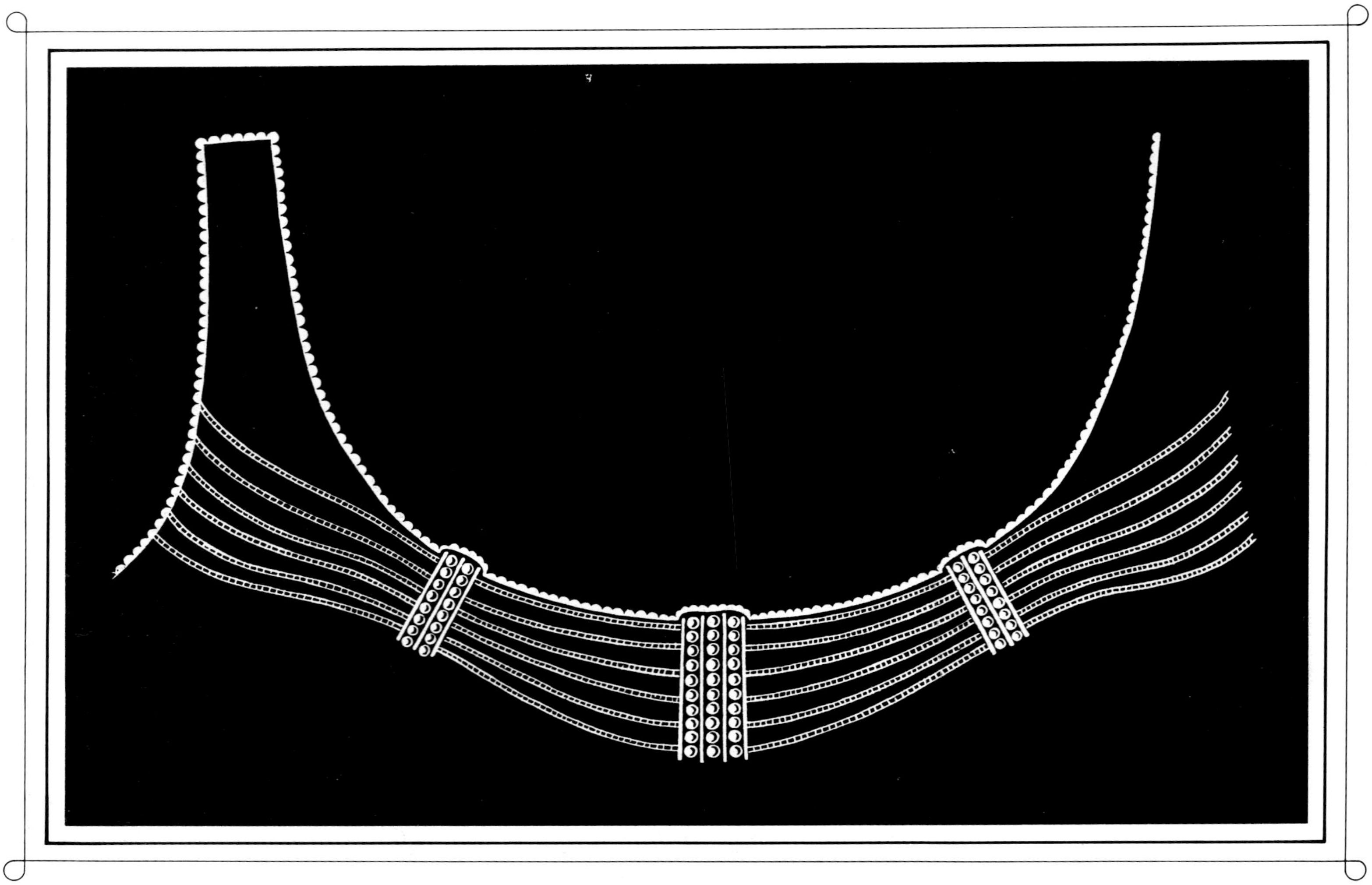

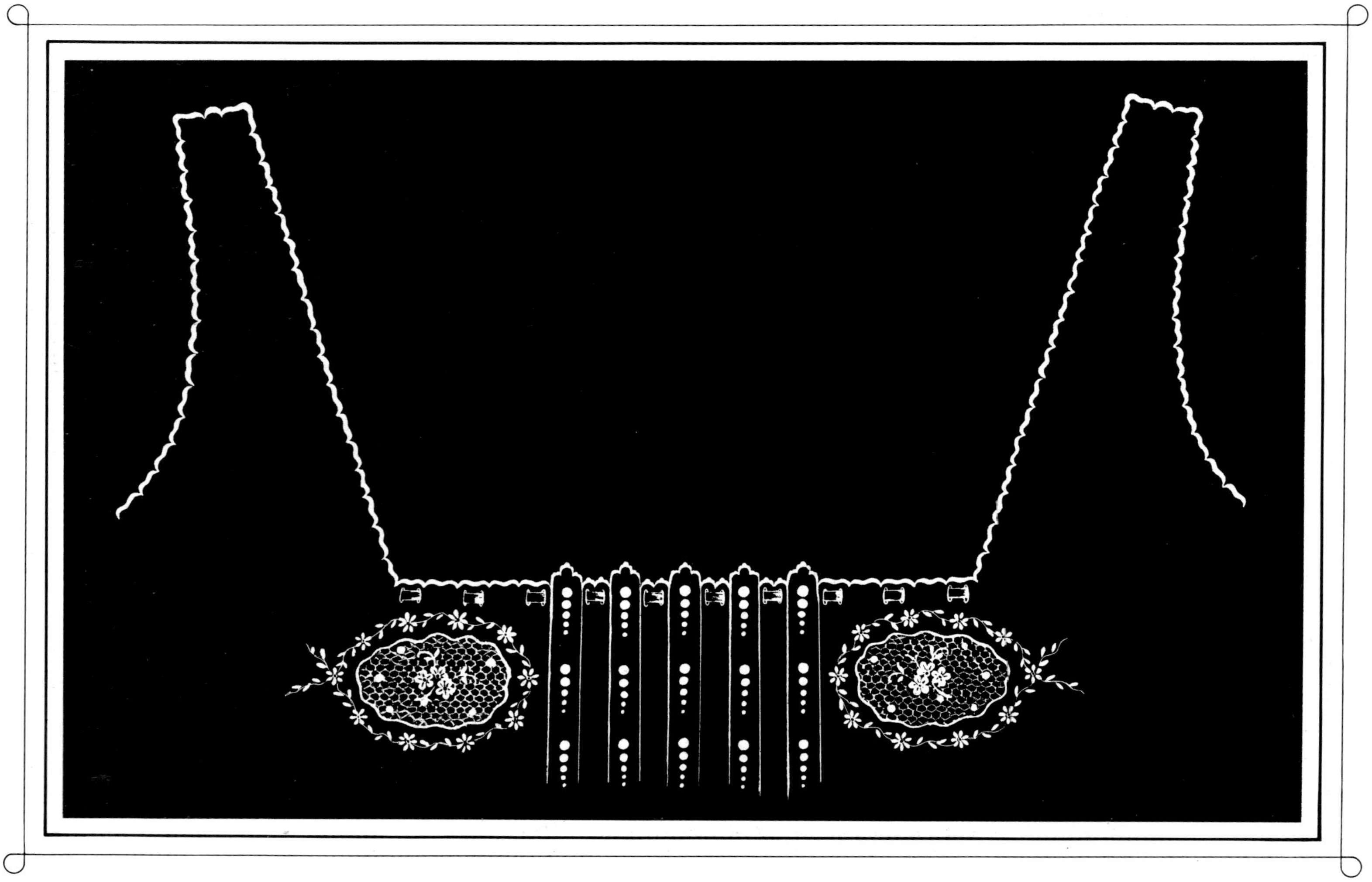

54

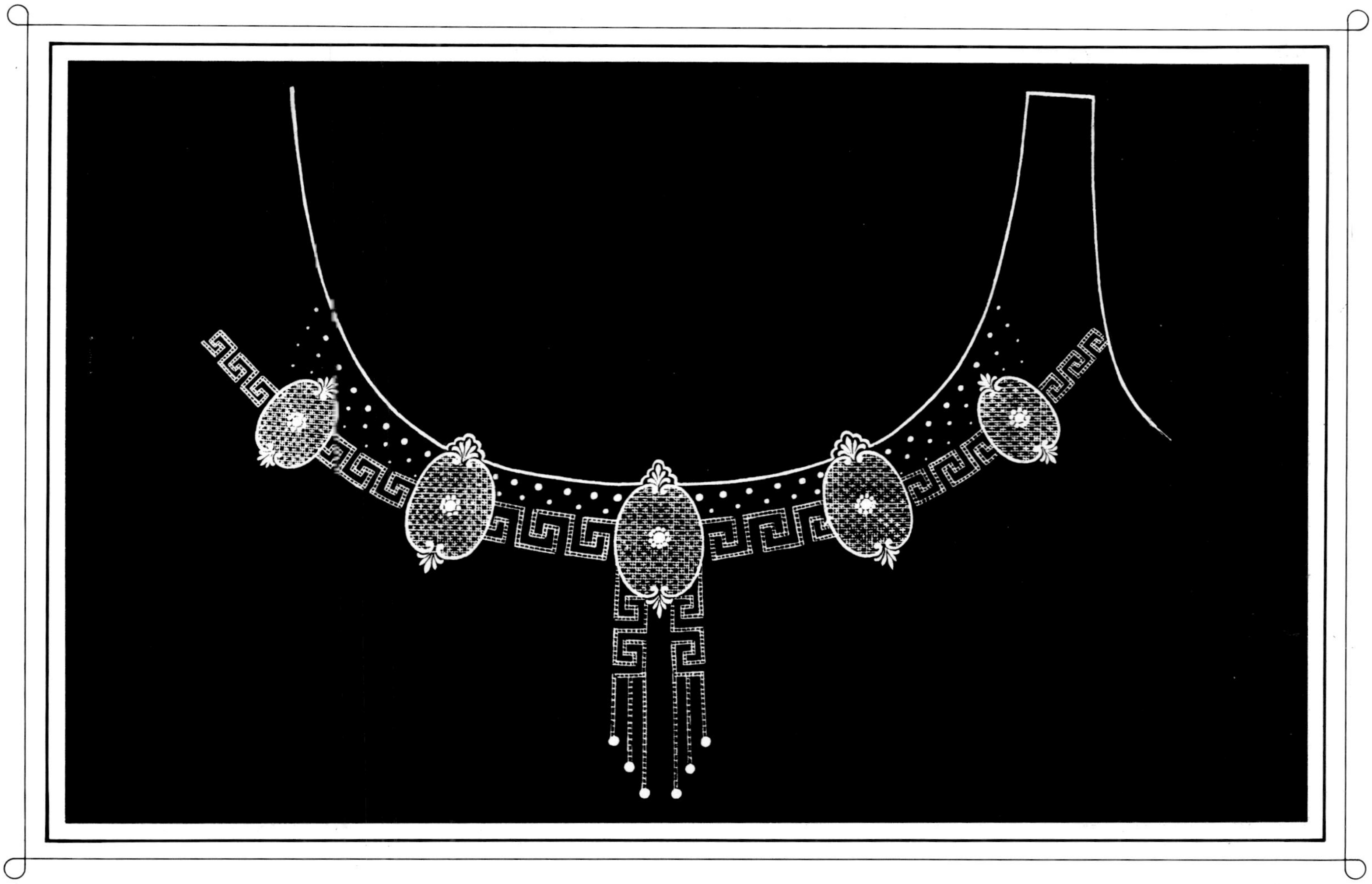

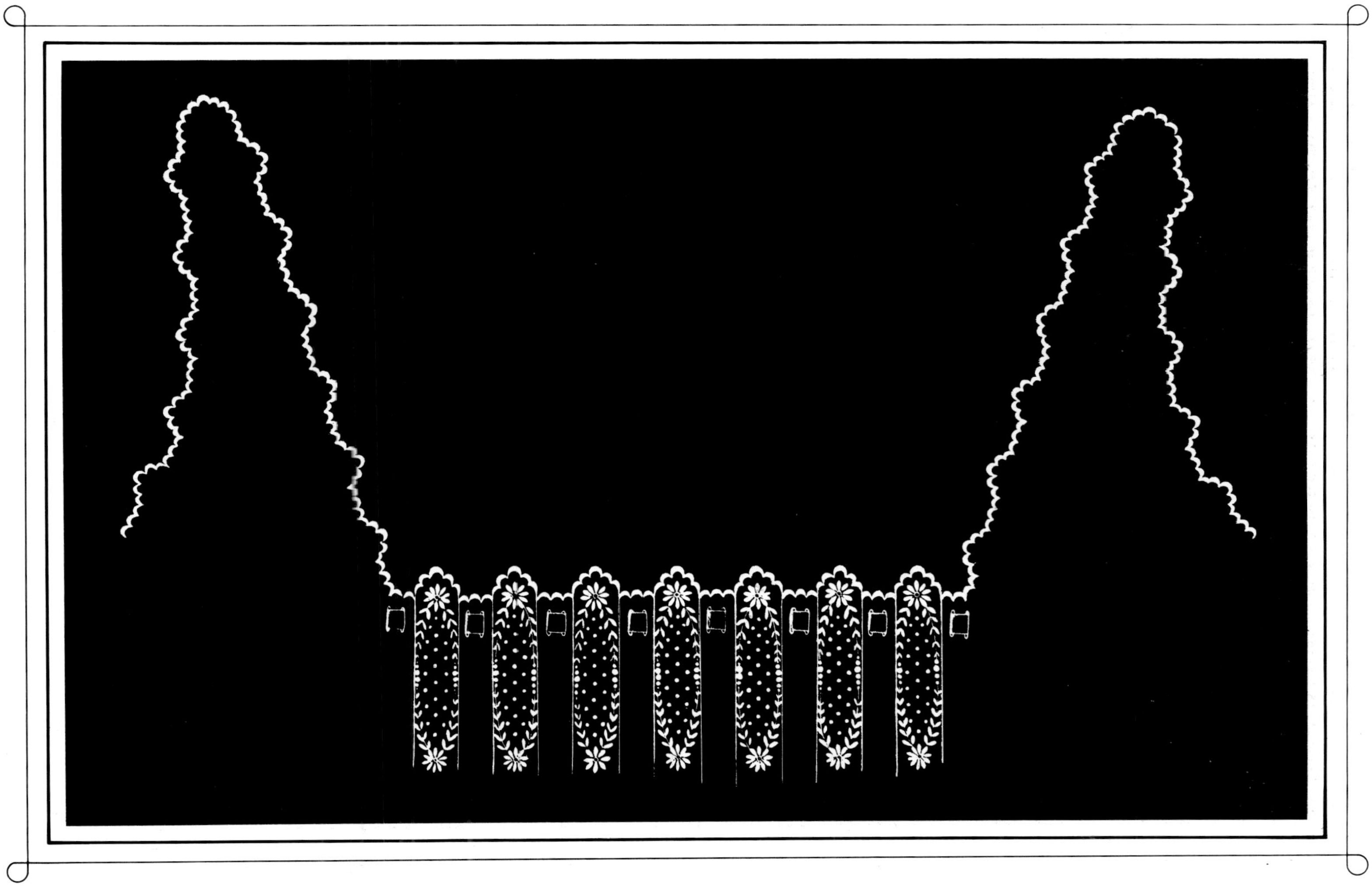

55

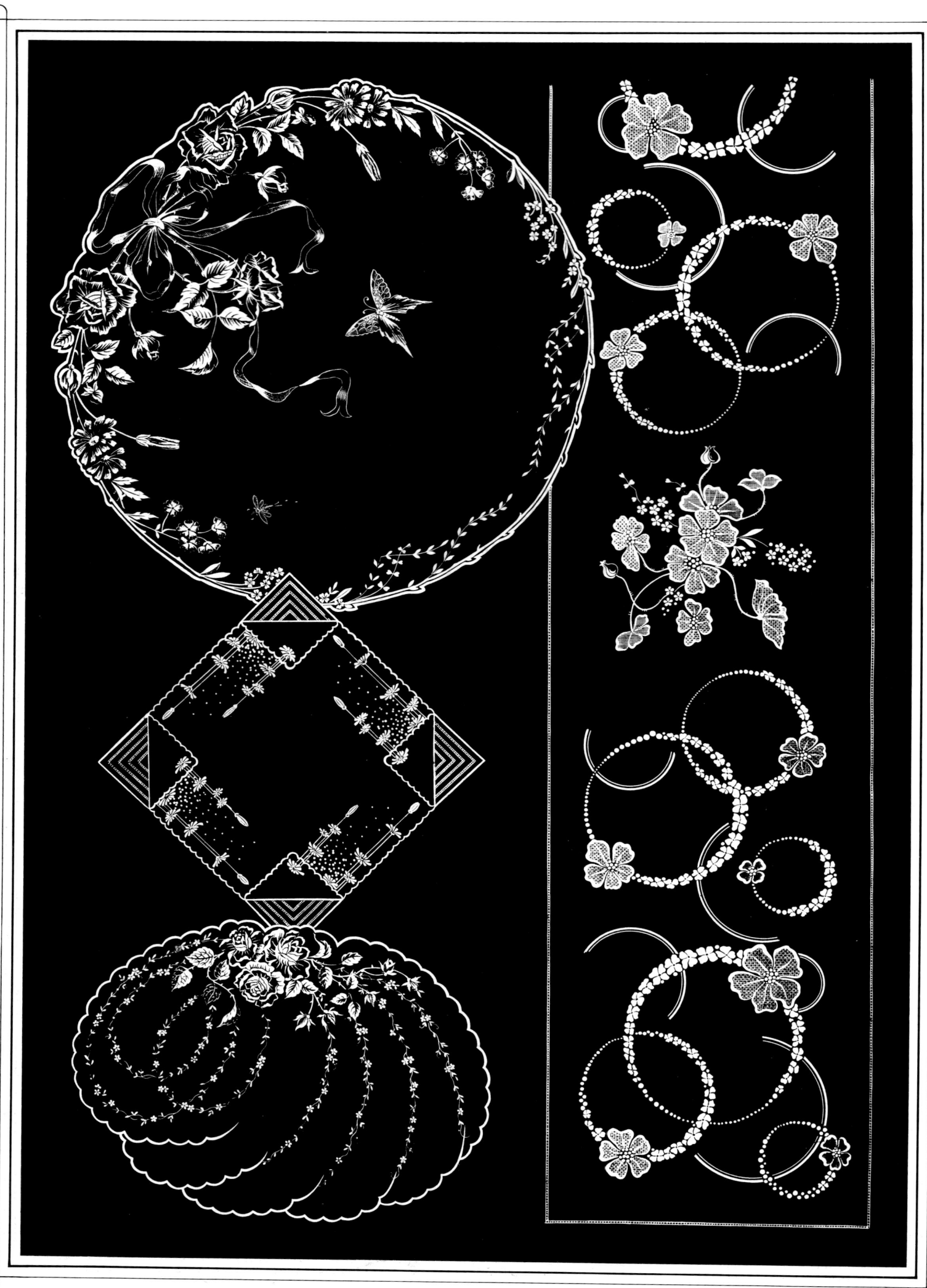

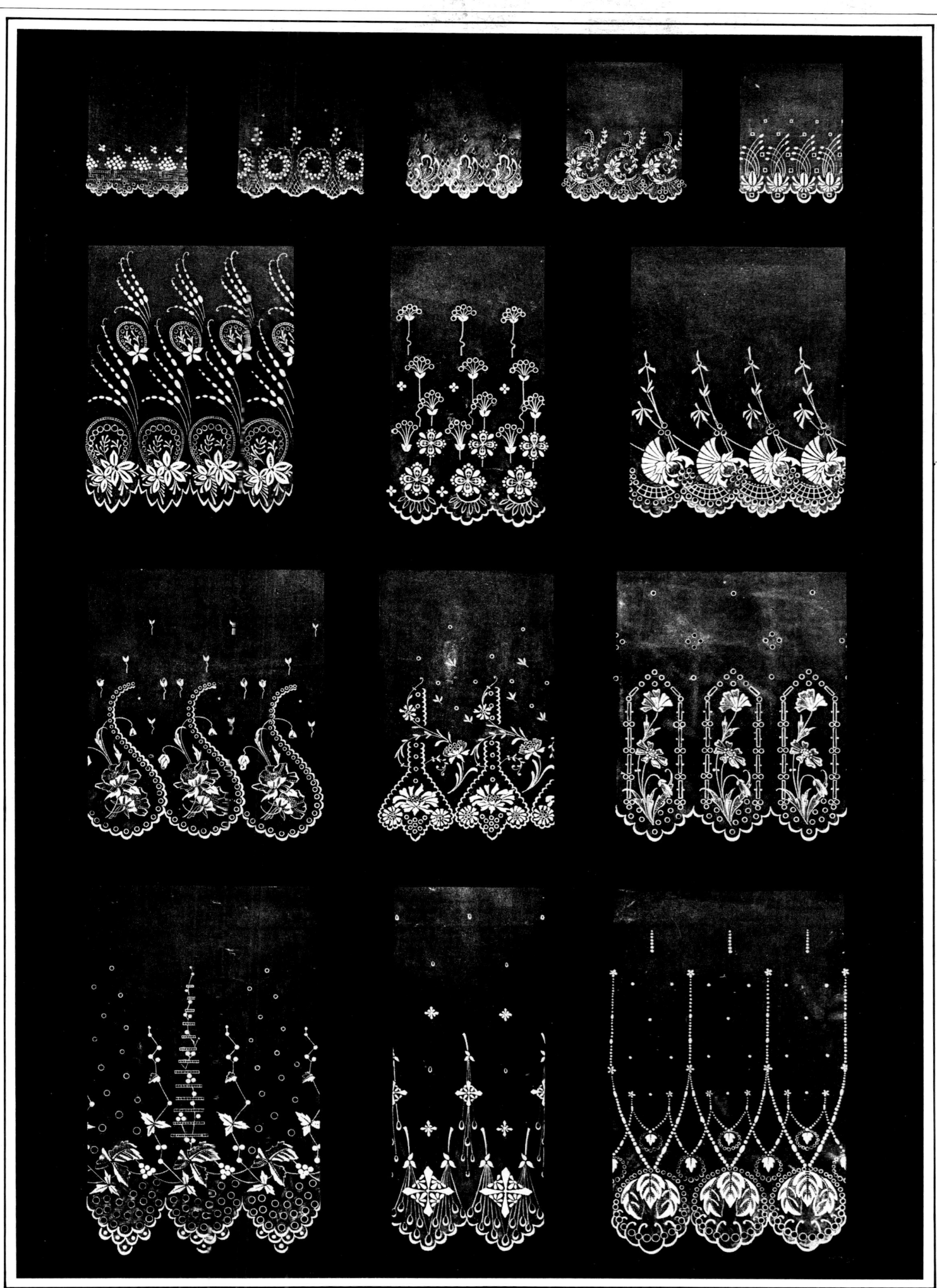

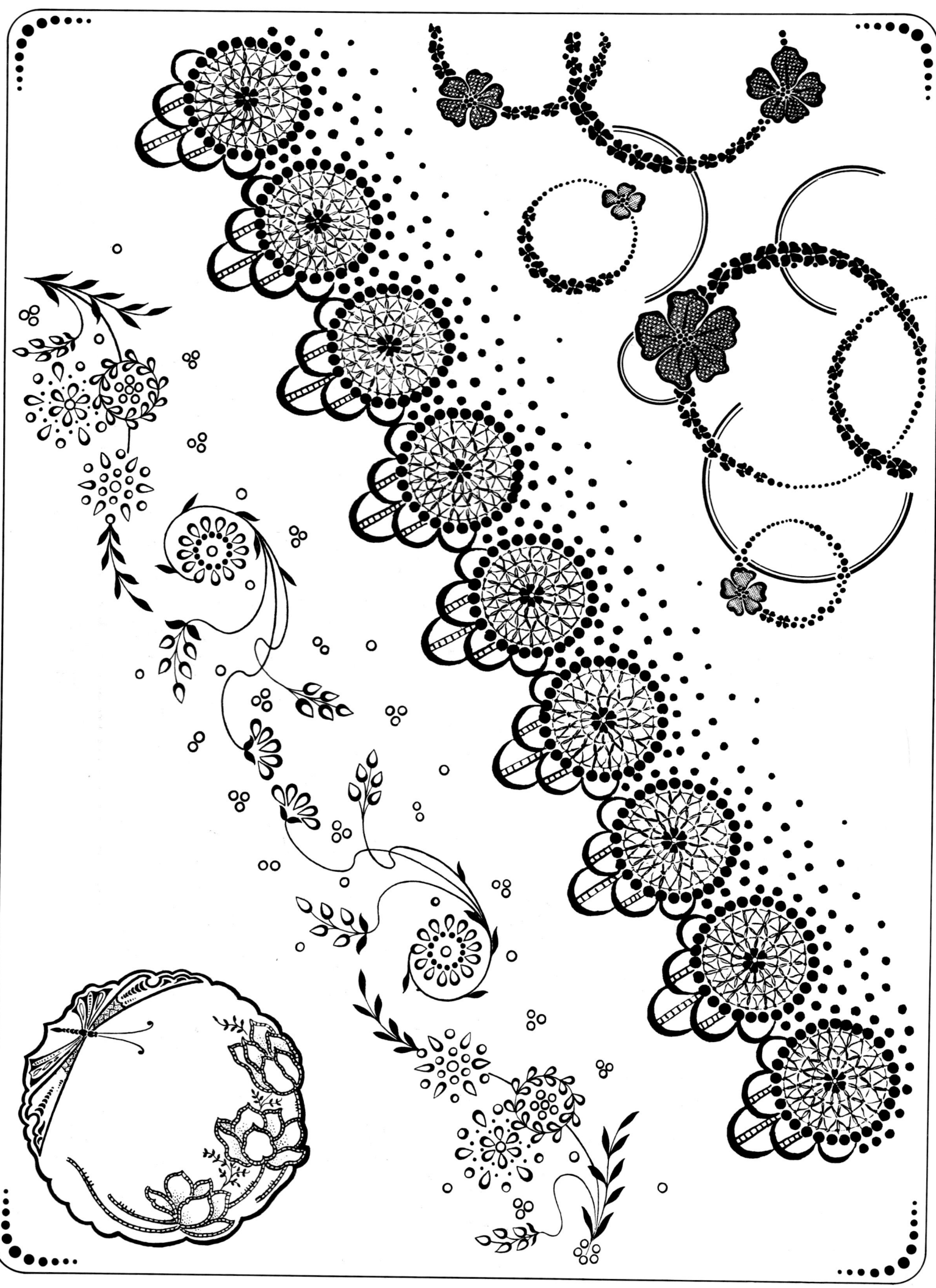

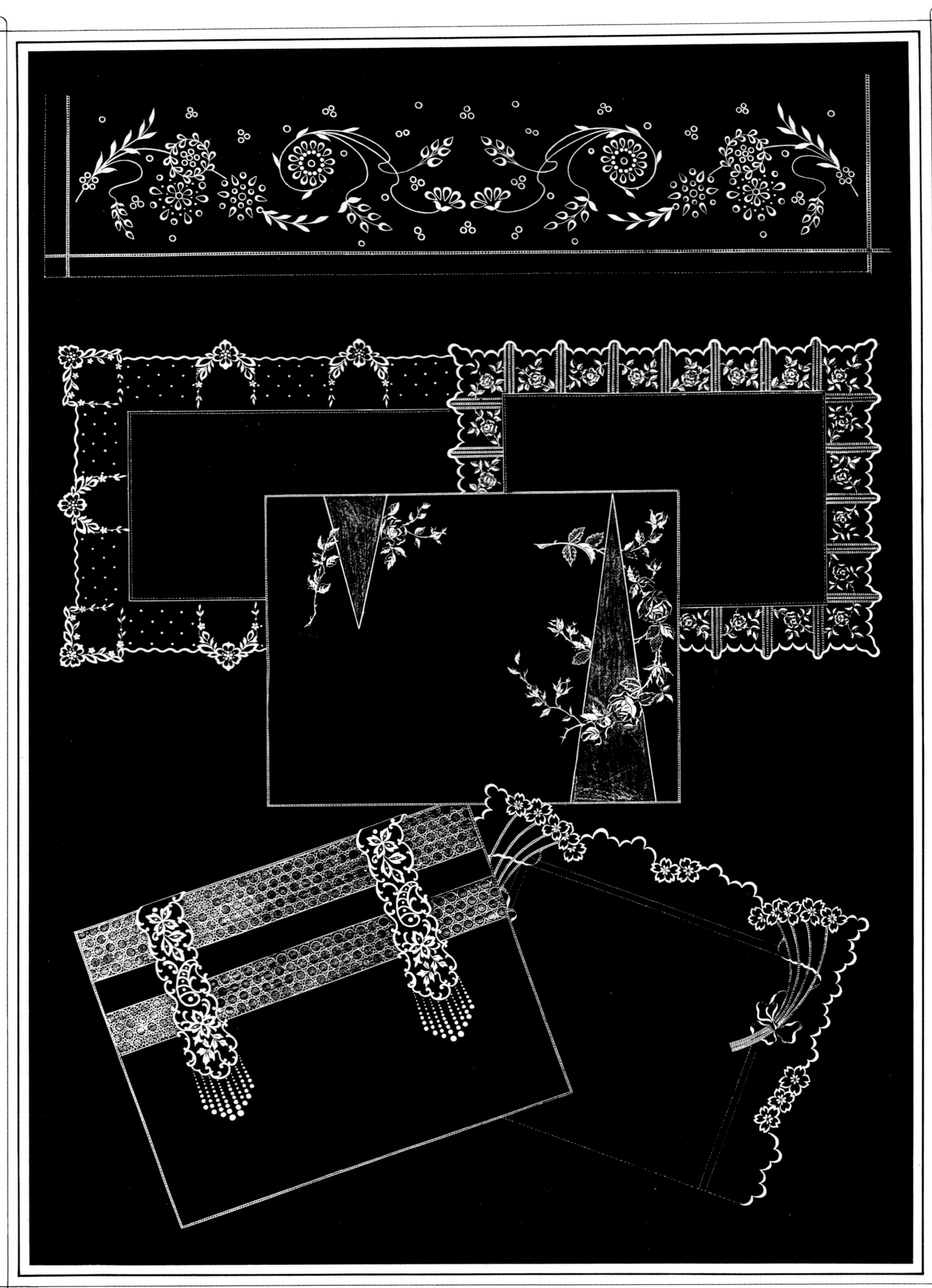

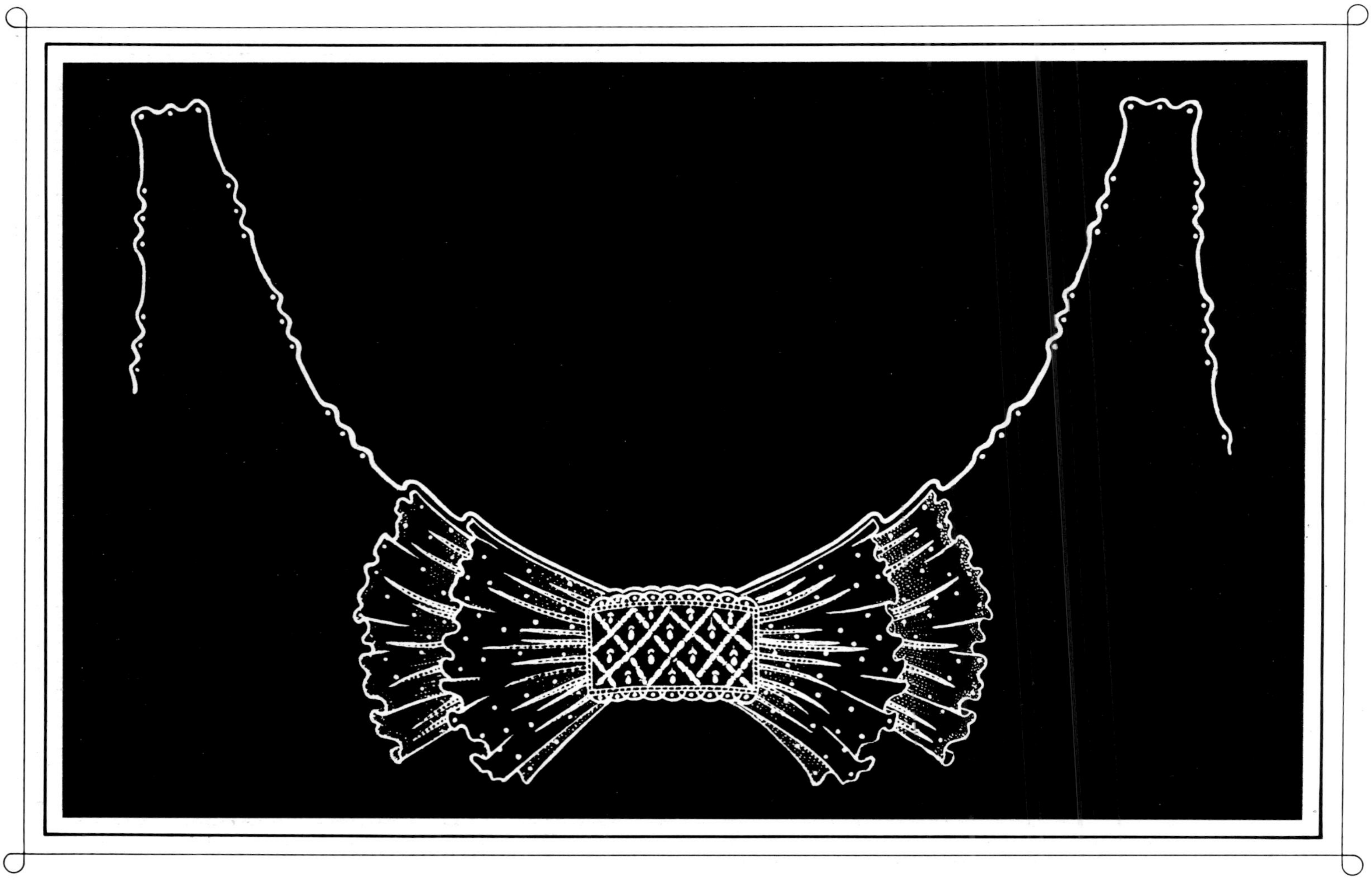

101

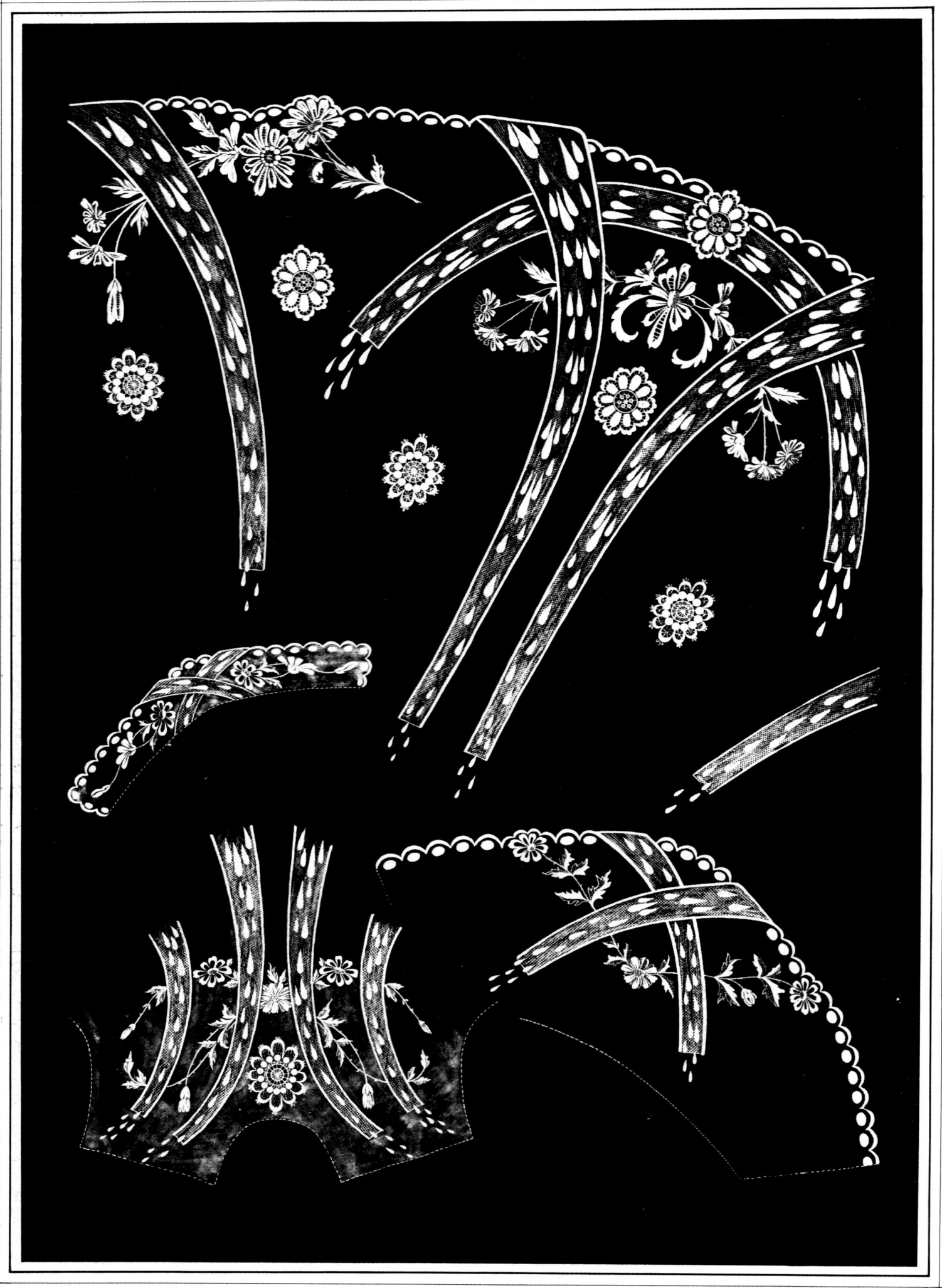

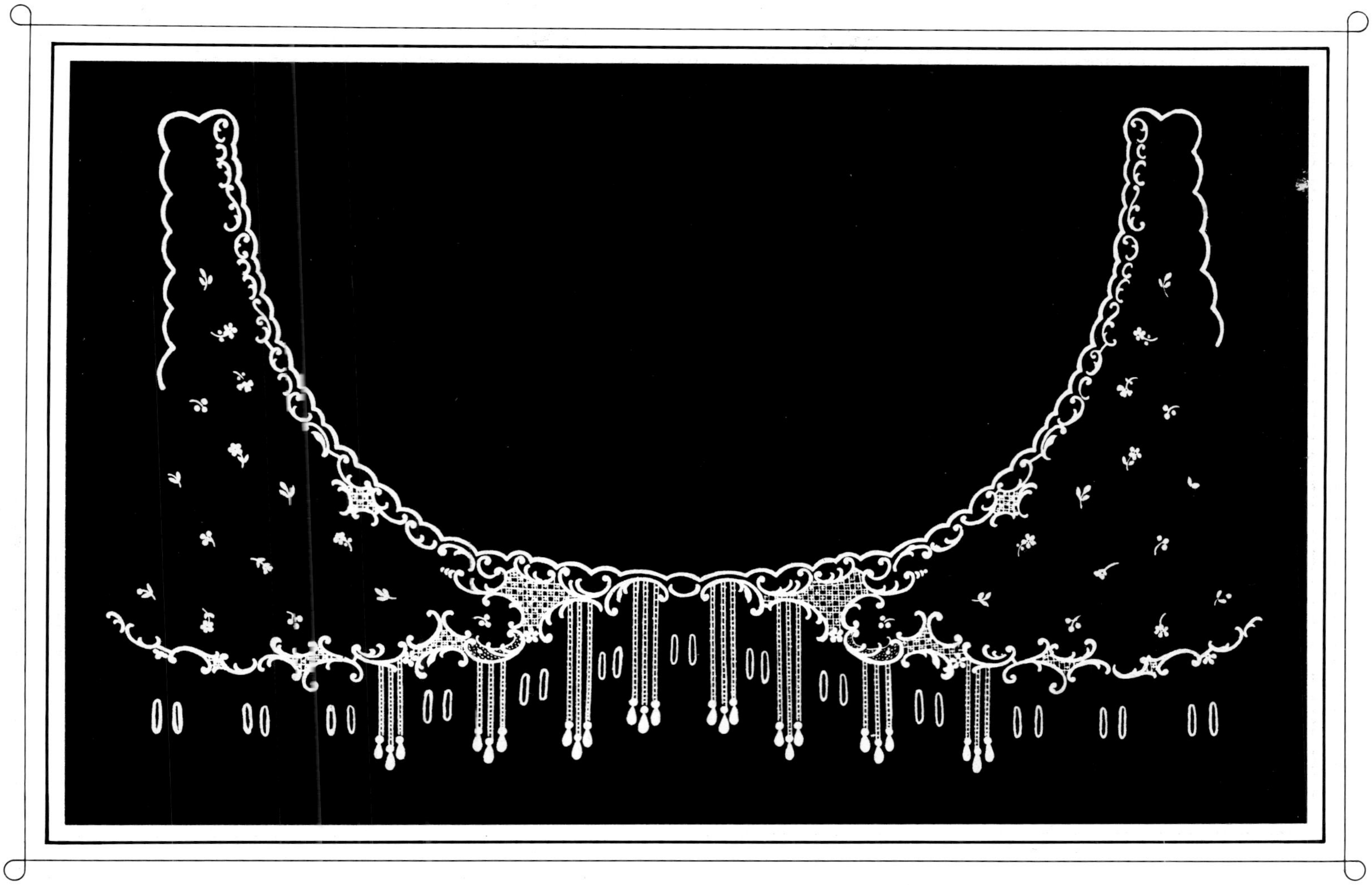

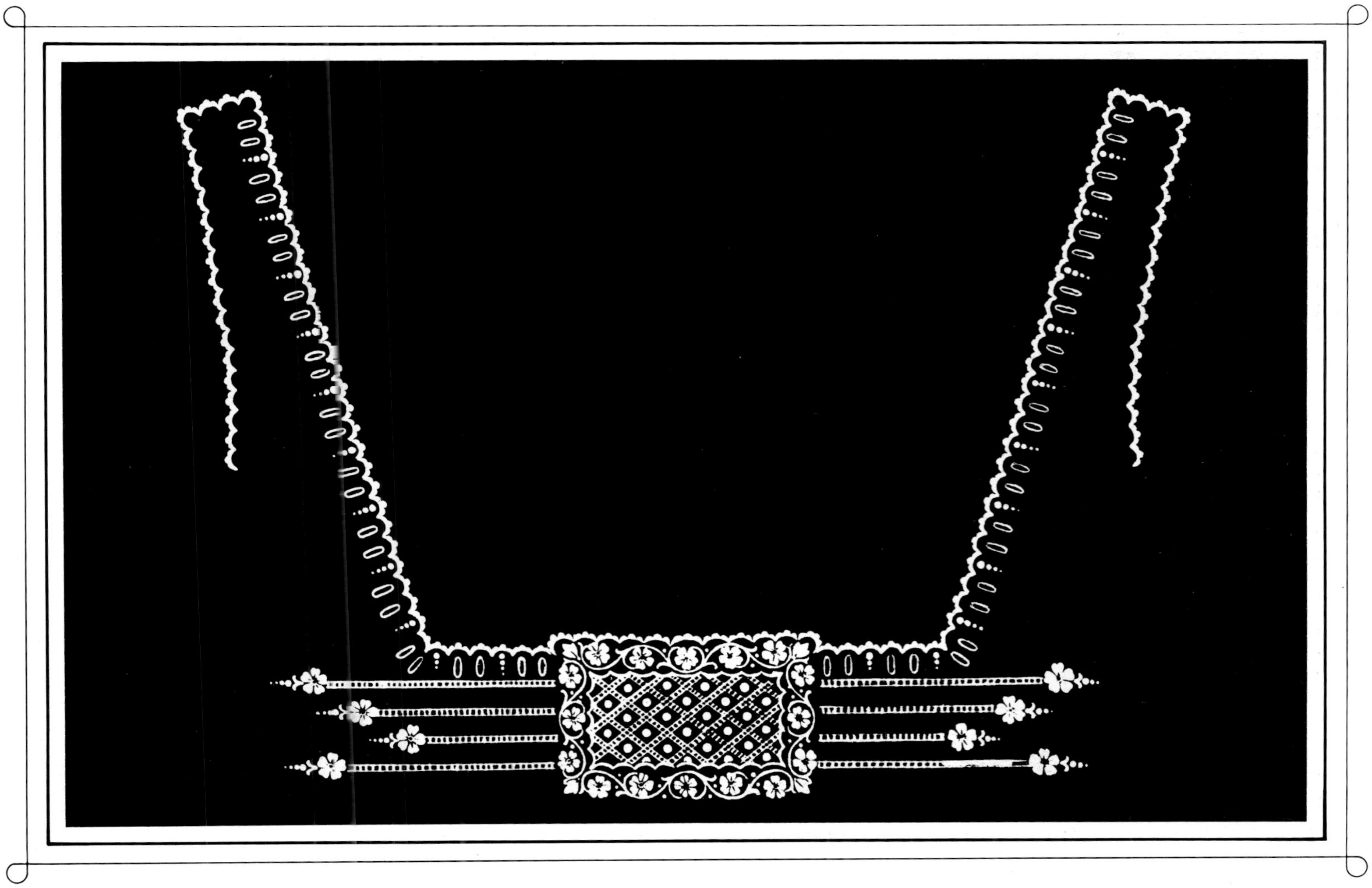

103

CREATIVE • DESIGN • IDEAS

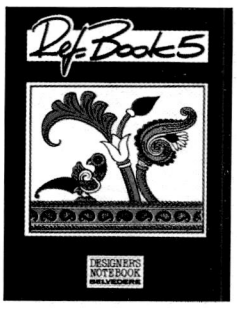     

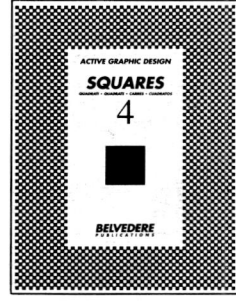     
    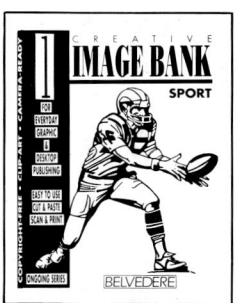 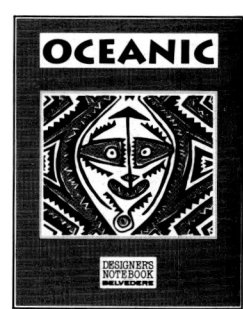

107

COLOR • SOURCE • BOOKS

  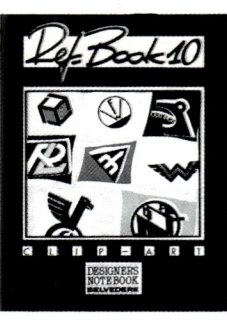   
   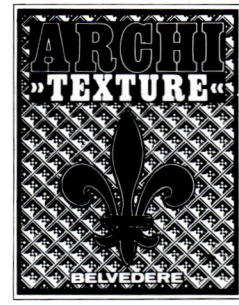  
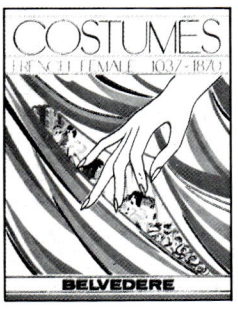     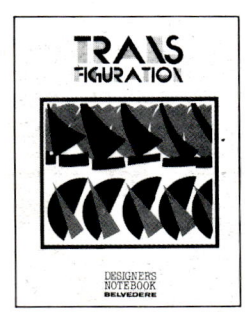

   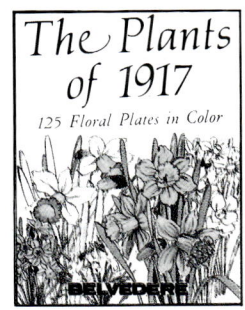  

PRACTICAL • GRAPHIC • ART

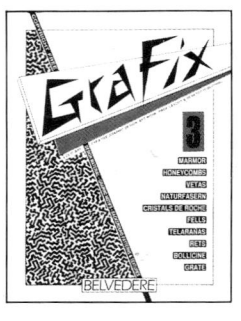     

 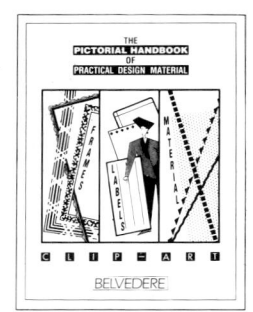   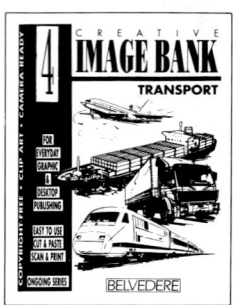 
     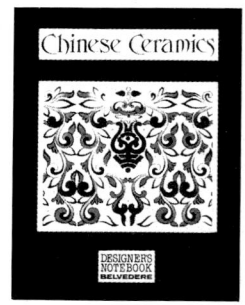

FASHION • TEXTILE • BOOKS

  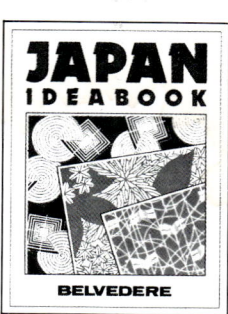  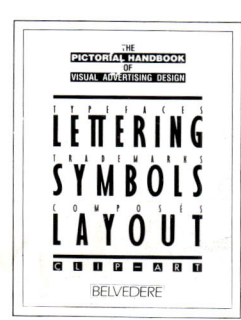 
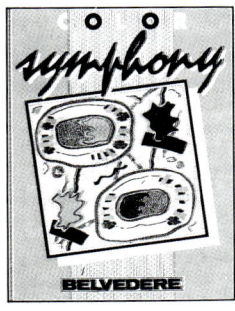 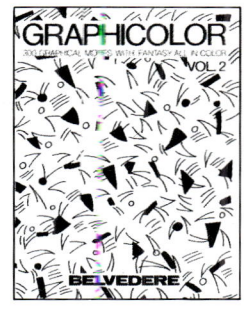 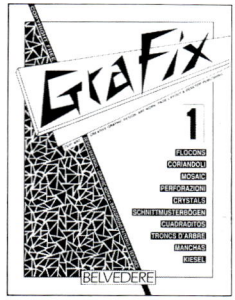  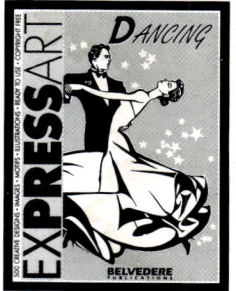 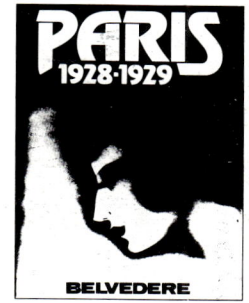
  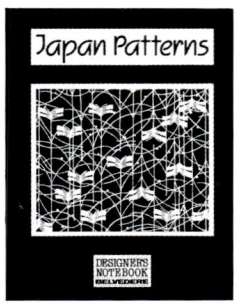  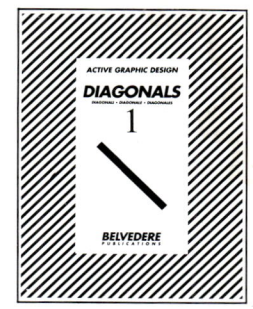 
 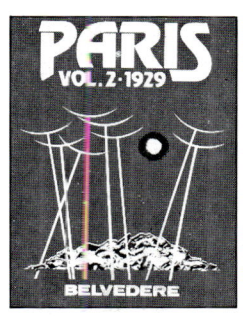   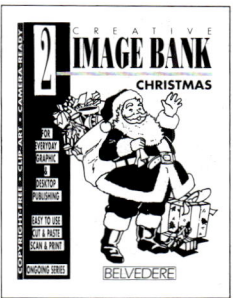 
 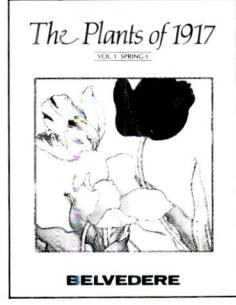   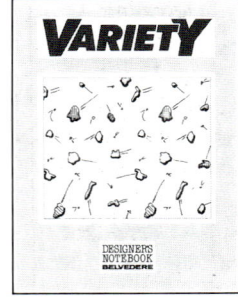 
  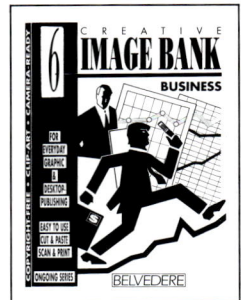 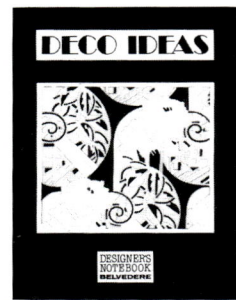  

If you want to be a member of the BELVEDERE DESIGN CLUB International...

▼

GOOD DESIGN BOOKS ARE HARD TO FIND. IT TAKES YOU TIME AND MONEY TO GET THE RIGHT IMAGES AND IDEAS, REFERENCES OR TOOLS YOU NEED FOR YOUR CREATIVE / PRACTICAL ART WORK. BUT NOW YOU CAN HAVE IT ALL MORE EASILY. CHOOSE SIMPLY THE BEST IN ITS FIELD: THE BELVEDERE-DESIGN-BOOKS, "MADE IN ITALY".
GO, AND ASK RIGHT NOW FOR THE "DESIGN CLUB" AND YOU WILL GET A VERY SPECIAL OFFER (FREE OF CHARGE) IMMEDIATELY. IT WILL SURPRISE YOU. WRITE, CALL OR FAX, OR SEND SIMPLY THE DESIGN-CLUB CARD TO ROME, ITALY FOR FURTHER INFORMATION OR FOR A FULL CATALOG. WE WILL DO ALL THE REST FOR YOU.

▼

É DIFFICILE TROVARE BUONI LIBRI DI DESIGN. CI VUOLE TEMPO E DENARO PER AVERE LE IMMAGINI E LE IDEE GIUSTE. MA ADESSO É TUTTO PIÚ FACILE. SCEGLIETE SOLAMENTE IL MEGLIO: I LIBRI • DESIGN DELLA EDIZIONE BELVEDERE, "MADE IN ITALY". CHIEDETE DEL DESIGN-CLUB INTERNATIONAL E AVRETE SUBITO GRATIS DELLE OFFERTE ECCEZIONALI CHE VI SORPRENDERANNO. MANDATE SEMPLICEMENTE LA CARTOLINA ACCANTO CON LA POSTA O VIA FAX PER RICEVERE ULTERIORI INFORMAZIONI O UN CATALOGO.

I N'EST PAS FACILE DE TROUVER DE BONS OUVRAGES DE DESSIN. VOUS AVEZ SANS DOUTE SOUVENT PERDU BEAUCOUP DE TEMPS ET D'ARGENT DANS LA RECHERCHE D'IMAGES & D'IDÉES NOUVELLES. AUJOURD'HUI CELA VOUS SERA PLUS FACILE. CHOISISSEZ TOUJOURS LE MEILLEUR: LES BELVEDERE DESIGN-BOOKS, "MADE IN ITALY". ÉCRIVEZ AU DESIGN-CLUB ET VOUS RECEVREZ GRATIS, ET PAR RETOUR DU CORRIER UNE OFFRE SPÉCIALE QUI VOUS SURPRENDERA AGRÉABLEMENT.

GUTE DESIGN BÜCHER SIND SCHWIERIG ZU FINDEN. ES ERFORDERT OFT VIEL ZEIT UND GELD, UM AN DIE RICHTIGEN IDEEN UND VORLAGEN ZU GELANGEN. DOCH JETZT IST DIES ALLES VIEL LEICHTER. WÄHLEN SIE EINFACH DAS BESTE: DIE BELVEDERE DESIGN-BÜCHER, "MADE IN ITALY". ERKUNDIGEN SIE SICH NACH DEM DESIGN-CLUB INTERNATIONAL UND SIE WERDEN UNVERZÜGLICH UND KOSTENLOS EIN SPEZIALANGEBOT ERHALTEN, DAS SIE ÜBERRASCHEN WIRD. ALLES ANDERE BESORGT FÜR SIE BELVEDERE.

ES REALMENTE DIFÍCIL ENCONTRAR BUENOS LIBROS DE DESIGN. SE NECESITAN TIEMPO Y DINERO PARA OBTENER LAS IMÁGENES & IDEAS APROPIADAS PARA VUESTRO TRABAJO. AHORA TODO ES MÁS FACIL. PUEDE CONSEGUIRSE LO MEJOR CON LOS BELVEDERE-DESIGN-BOOKS, "MADE IN ITALY". ES SUFICIENTE SOLICITARLOS AL DESIGN-CLUB INTERNACIONAL; INMEDIATAMENTE, Y GRATIS, RECIBIRÉIS MERAVILLOSAS OFERTAS.

▼